The Sarah Maguire Prize
2020

The Sarah Maguire Prize 2020

Judged by Alireza Abiz, Leo Boix
and Ida Hadjivayanis

poetry
translation
centre

First published in 2021
by the Poetry Translation Centre Ltd
The Albany, Douglas Way, London, SE8 4AG

www.poetrytranslation.org

Introduction © Alireza Abiz

ISBN: 978-1-9161141-6-6

A catalogue record for this book is available from the British Library

Typeset in Minion / Nassim Arabic / Source Han Serif
by Poetry Translation Centre Ltd / WorldAccent

Cover Design: Kit Humphrey
Printed in the UK by TJ Books Limited

The PTC is supported using public funding by
Arts Council England

Contents

Introduction

In her fourth poetry collection, *The Pomegranates of Kandahar* (2007), Sarah Maguire included the poem 'From Dublin to Ramallah', which is dedicated to the Palestinian poet Ghassan Zaqtan – a poet she had helped to translate into English. In the poem she writes:

I call for a liquid dissolution:
Let borders dissolve, let words dissolve,
Let English absorb the fluency of Arabic, with ease

I notice how, in this vivid, lyric expression of her fury at the physical borders separating people, Sarah quickly turned to the linguistic barriers and, with characteristic force of will, commanded poetry to flow from one language into another. This seems fitting for a poet who dedicated much of her life and time to bringing poetry from so many other languages into English.

When Sarah founded the Poetry Translation Centre in 2004, one of her aims was 'to ginger up poetry in English through translating contemporary poetry from Africa, Asia and Latin America'. She worked toward this goal tirelessly until her death in 2017 and managed to bring leading poets from around the world to English audiences through collaboration between dozens of poets and translators. She had first become seriously interested in translation when she was sent to Palestine by the British Council in 1996. There Sarah discovered poetry of a totally different nature; a poetry which was at the centre of cultural and political life. She worked with linguists to translate contemporary poets she felt particularly passionate about and this became the pattern that she would later employ in the PTC workshops. This collaborative process of bringing together a translator's linguistic expertise with an English-language poet's skill formed the basis of the PTC's approach for many years and created some dazzling translations. Thanks to Sarah's vision, the PTC is now a major force for bringing exciting contemporary poetry from languages and cultures historically underrepresented in English and for engaging with a diverse plethora of diaspora communities in the UK.

Sarah trained as a gardener and I like to imagine that she treated the translation of poetry with the same passion and tenderness that a horticulturist brings to introducing beautiful foreign plants to their garden. She worked hard to pair poets and translators and create translations which had a poetic character in English while being faithful to the meaning in the original language. In doing so, she enriched and increased the poetic vocabulary of the English language – as well, of course, as her own. Sarah argued that '[all the major] revolutions in English poetry have occurred via translation, when poets have unequivocally embraced what is distant and unfamiliar. English poetry simply wouldn't be English poetry without poets absorbing influences from abroad'. She saw translating poetry into English as a service to English poetry and an English poetry audience, just as much as it was a service to the language being translated.

It is within this context and as a way to celebrate the lasting legacy of Sarah Maguire that the PTC and Sarah's friends and family came together to establish the Sarah Maguire Prize for Poetry in Translation. This new biennial prize aims to recognise and promote the best book of poetry translated into English from a living poet from Africa, Asia, Latin America or the Middle East. The books can be published anywhere in the world and the winning collection will receive a prize of £3,000 to be shared equally between the poet and their translator or translators.

In this, the first year of running the prize, the PTC received submissions from 24 countries and 18 different languages. The cultural and linguistic diversity of the submissions promised an exciting journey for me and the other two judges – Leo Boix and Ida Hadjivayanis. Our aim was simple enough in theory, we were to choose the best submissions as in any other competition, but how could we define what's best in an area as contested and varied as poetry in translation? The aim of the prize was commendably broad and we wanted to ensure that no single attitude towards what constitutes good poetry or good translation practice dominated at the expense of others. But, in the spirit of Sarah, we took our initiative from the PTC's workshops and sought translations that we perceived to be as close as possible to the original poet's intentions, while also being effective poems in English. Viewing translation of poetry as a collaboration, we were interested in the input of all parties to this collaboration; the culture and poetic tradition of the original as well as the final product in the English language. We wanted to choose titles which were important books in themselves, opened windows to a different culture and could also be read as great poetry in English; translations that 'worked' and could, in Sarah's words, 'ginger up' English poetry.

As expected, the process was both joyful and agonising. Joyful as we came across so many exciting poets from languages and poetic cultures that we knew little about and agonising as we could choose only a handful. Yet, strangely enough, when comparing notes in the first of several meetings we found we'd independently selected very similar shortlists. Despite our initial fears that we'd agreed to judge an unjudgeable competition, likely to be fraught with unreconciled arguments, we found the process surprisingly simple. The shortlisted titles had stood out for all of us. All of them had one thing in common: great poetry that had been beautifully translated. I am no closer to offering a definition of 'great poetry' than I was when I agreed to judge the competition and yet I'm certain that each of the shortlisted titles offers us – as readers of English – that greatness. A gift that can be made to us only through the brilliance of their translators. That these books appealed so immediately and lastingly to all three judges – from three very different linguistic and literary backgrounds – is perhaps the best measure of their power.

The first of the shortlisted titles presented here, *A Boat to Lesbos and other poems* by Nouri Al-Jarrah and translated from the Arabic by Camilo Gómez-Rivas and Allison Blecker, invites the reader to experience the unbearable agony of hopelessness in the face of the most brutal events of our time. From the first line, the title poem calls upon us to see what we have tried so hard to look away from:

> Suffering Syrians, beautiful Syrians, Syrian brothers fleeing death. You won't reach the shores on rafts but will be born on beaches with the foam.
> Lost gold dust you are, melted gold dust, scattered, dulled.

A Boat to Lesbos is a contemporary epic borrowing from the ancient Greek tragedies to witness the plight of millions of Syrians trying to escape violence by crossing the Mediterranean Sea to reach Europe. There is no hero or heroine in this epic. There is no heroism, no action or invitation to any action. The poems do not look like experiences in language and on paper. They are living witnesses in flesh and blood to the most horrific experiences of an entire nation. The book is a show of unparalleled despair in the face of the dignified suffering of the poet's compatriots where the only thing he can do is to carve their stories on 'the rocks of pain'.

> Like mermaids born in the quivering light, beautiful Syrian women set tender, wounded soles on the rocks and grey sand of Lesbos.

> Come down from the fruits of al-Sham to the rocks of pain.

Al-Jarrah's poignant use of different voices, his preference for short lines and brief scattered stanzas, help to infuse the book with a sense of clarity and transparency. The book, translated with much attention to detail and also beautifully illustrated, succeeds as a poetical project by incorporating other poems into the main sequence adding to a sense of loss, injustice and human desperation, and yet never sentimentalising the topic.

Factory Girls by Takako Arai, translated from the Japanese by Jeffrey Angles, Jen Crawford, Carol Hayes, Rina Kikuchi, You Nakai and Sawako Nakayasu, offers a vivid depiction of the world of women workers in Japan's textile industry. The poet herself grew up in and around a small silk-weaving factory owned by her father and many of the poems in this collection are about the lives of the women workers she knew from that time. In an intense narrative, she talks about the factory environment, the machinery, the work routines and the lasting impact of the factory on the women's lives. She manages to convey some of her main themes and preoccupations, such as the deindustrialisation of Japan and the impacts of economic decline in post-industrial cities in a fresh and exciting voice which is full of surprises on different levels, be it diction, imagery, pace, rhythm and tone. Poems' titles, such as 'Bobbins', 'Wheels', 'Beds and Looms', 'Nylon Scarf', and 'the Healds', act as the starting point for narratives not only about those objects but also about the lives of the people who touched them, operated them, repaired them or made them.

The collection's opening poem, 'When the Moon Rises', exemplifies Arai's skill in setting up a seemingly straightforward narrative, here about an abandoned spinning factory:

It is the night shift in an abandoned spinning factory
There is only a single light bulb here
The spools of thread turn by themselves
Click goes the bobbins
Changed by the machines
A decade has already gone by
Since this place shut down
But when the moon rises, it begins to work

Only for the poem to trace, with finely woven lyric and intellectual nuance, its living legacy:

Peculiar habits remain here
An old lady who spun thread
For forty-four years here
Still licks her index finger and twists
Even on her deathbed
She cannot escape the gesture
That must be true in the netherworld too
Since threads are so infinitely thin
Gestures sink into the bodies
Of those who manipulated the machines
And possesses them.

In Fawzi Karim's *Incomprehensible Lesson*, in versions by Anthony Howell working after translations from the Arabic made by the author, the poet writes about his homeland, exile and the very sense of belonging. Karim reveals conflicting sentiments toward his Iraqi homeland and his Arabic poetry tradition. His relationship with his homeland is not that of a loving nostalgia, as is the case of many exiled poets. Instead it is agonised, painful and hurt. He loses his homeland twice, once when he left to start a life in exile and again when he returned, after the end of dictatorship, only to find out that his 'home' was no longer there. The city of his youth does not remember him and that nothing is left to remind him of himself. His poems act to restore his homeland from the remnants of his memory with the help of imagination. Throughout Karim's mournful poems are wonderfully captured in Howell's lyrical phrasing. 'The Forgotten City' can be read as a metaphorical representation of this lost homeland:

10

The birds have flown, their nests abandoned.
And you too, you out-of-place Tuareg,
You've left nothing but footprints.
Come to the waves too late,
you've stared at them too long.

Echoes of footfalls… leaves in a whirl…
Once a scorcher burnt the wrist of this metropolis.
Now it has cooled to a bracelet of silver
Worn just the once, an age ago, by some forgetful girl.

This collection explores, with a luminous touch, the ethical and political aspects of exile.

Kim Yideum's *Hysteria*, translated from the Korean by Jake Levine, Soeun Seo and Hedgie Choi is an unusually exciting poetry collection. Its lively, confrontational, energetic and down-to-earth language serves a poet with a pitch-black sense of humour and a gift for narrative. Kim writes with an exceptional ease about a wide range of everyday topics and different sentiments moving from fury to laughter, the humorous to the tragic, in a single poem. The book is an experimental exploration of the self in all its forms, through the clever use of irony and elements of surrealism to convey a sense of uneasiness, bitterness and vulnerability. The poet adopts countless personas and voices, often employing a seemingly confessional tone in poems which also ridicule the act of confession or render it pointless. The title poem, 'Hysteria', like many other poems in the book, can be read in multiple ways. We can even start to read it as prose:

I want to rip you apart with my teeth. I want to tear you to
death on this speeding subway. Hey, you groping, hey, hey,
hands off! I feel like I'm ripping, like I'll tear apart every second.
I want to scream, throw a fit, but I take my hand and push
deep into my gut. Breath. Deep. Don't fucking touch me. I
said stop leaning on me. You're driving me nuts, what the fuck?

The poem's title is thrown into question – the speaker's rage prompted by the experience of being groped on public transport is justified and understandable and has all-too-often historically been dismissed as the imagination of a hysteric. But the poem is not touting for sympathy, it explores the extremes of feelings with astonishing freedom and off-beat humour:

I want to kill the
motherfucker. But what if he's my lover? If only I could pick
him up by the back of his neck with my teeth. I would leap off
this train and sprint over the tracks. I would head to the darkest

part of the night, my wild hair flapping. If only I could go to
the sandy beach on the red coast, moonlit. There, beside the
cool waters, I would lay him down. If only.

Tiawanaku, Poems from the Mother Coqa by Judith Santopietro, translated from
the Spanish by Ilana Luna, charts a journey into the geography and history of
the indigenous Andean territories and offers a reimagining of ancient Latin
American cultures, languages and spiritualities. It is a fascinating representation
of indigenous people and their relationship with their environment. The poet uses
oral traditions of poetry and storytelling as well as her lived experience to portray
the struggle for cultural and linguistic survival in the face of an inherited colonial
past and increasing globalisation.

The book is politically significant and pressingly relevant as it documents
the damage to the cultural and linguistic diversity of Latin America as a result
of imperialistic policies. By taking us through the mountains and valleys and the
rituals and spiritual practices, the book reminds us of the cruelty of policies that
are still at work today to marginalise indigenous nations and impose various forms
of discrimination against them. In a poem titled 'Kalasasaya', we read:

And yet the vertical stones in this grassland
the air inhabiting the passageways
stone faces in an ochre-walled temple

Even still   I stretch my arms beyond where I can see:
I fall from this peak
I hold the blade in one hand
                    with the other   I feel the heart and its roar
                    I hold back the injuries that erode my mouth

this is the land where I wasn't born
its dusty parade wearies me
I'm indifferent to its empires of racism

Yang Lian's *Anniversary Snow*, primarily translated from the Chinese by Brian
Holton with additional translations by W.N. Herbert, L. Leigh, Pascale Petit, Fiona
Sampson, George Szirtes and Joshua Weiner, is yet another fascinating collection.
The book is grounded in the historical roots of Chinese culture, poetry and art,
but goes far beyond it, reinterpreting with poise and intelligence the very essence
of our existence, from the changing landscape that surrounds us, the appeal of the
natural world and the inner beauty of language, exemplifying its political force
and its philosophical teachings. Each poem in this collection can amaze the reader
in a unique way. The imagery throughout is sophisticated and enigmatic. In many
poems, we find Yang in dialogue with other poets – both key Chinese poets of past

centuries as well as wide array of contemporary international poets. In 'Advanced Study', dedicated to the great Syrian poet Adonis, Yang seems to be speaking about and beyond poetry as he writes:

> a poem   destroyed is indestructibly alive
> a tiny hexagon can't go past   its
> tongue snags on the world   its dribbling more than the world
> a little window props one side of us up as we walk leaning together
> choosing not to shoot as you pull the trigger like a DDR soldier picking a word
>   in a poem
> scribbling into an elegy that transcends every death that has ever been
> BC at both ends of a verse   suffering utterly red   pinching
>   One more suck holds the Sunday anniversary
> a silvery white recording   stings the all-pervading
> heart spasms once and has won history

> a poem waits until the dead come lifelike back

Anniversary Snow is a multi-layered, lyrically complex collection that reflects Yang's myriad preoccupations as an artist, including exile, flows of migration, artistic friendships, the power of art, history, music and language, as well as the endless source of inspiration drawn from Chinese culture.

Taken together, the six shortlisted titles provide a splendid panorama of the poetry being written in different languages and cultures today. This poetic diversity is mirrored by the variety of translation approaches that are showcased on the shortlist. Translation is always a collaboration and contemporary poetic translation thrives on the connections that new means of communications make ever more available. Many translators work in direct contact with the poets they translate. Despite achieving the seamless quality of a voice in English, the two translators of *A Boat to Lesbos* gratefully note the suggestions received from a number of other poets and translators and the text benefits further from its illustrations. Six different translators were involved in translating *Factory Girls* and many of the individual poems are the outcome of the collaborative work of more than one translator. The poems in *Incomprehensible Lesson* are introduced as 'versions by Anthony Howell after translations made by the author' and demonstrate the fruit of close collaboration between two poets. While the majority of the poems in *Anniversary Snow* are translated by Brian Holton, the book also includes translations by English-language poets who don't know Chinese and have produced translations through a process that Yang Lian calls 'poet-to-poet' translation. Ilana Luna, the translator of *Tiawanaku* notes the deeply collaborative experience of translating the book in her introduction and notes the importance of her editor's role in the process. In *Hysteria* the three translators – Jake Levine, Soeun Seo and Hedgie Choi – worked together on each and every poem. This emphasis on the collaborative approach to translation demonstrated by the shortlist is heartening and feels in keeping with Sarah Maguire's memory. It underlines the will to connect that ignites poetry and translation alike.

Alireza Abiz
Chair of the Judges, 2020

Nouri Al-Jarrah

A Boat
to Lesbos

and other poems

Translated from the Arabic
by Camilo Gómez-Rivas
and Allison Blecker

Banipal 𝐁𝐁 Books

A Boat to Lesbos and other poems

by Nouri Al-Jarrah
Translated from the Arabic by Camilo Gómez-Rivas and Allison Blecker
Banipal Books; 2018

The title poem of Syrian poet Nouri Al-Jarrah's *A Boat to Lesbos and other poems* is a powerful epic written while thousands of Syrian refugees were enduring frightening journeys across the Mediterranean before arriving on the shores of the small Greek island of Lesbos. Set out like a Greek tragedy, the poem is a passionate and dramatic witness to the horrors and ravages suffered by Syrian families forced to flee their destroyed country, but seen through the eye of history, the poetry of Sappho and the travels of Odysseus.

'A Boat to Lesbos', originally published in Arabic as *Qarib ila Lesbos*, in 2016, with this English edition translated by Camilo Gómez-Rivas and Allison Blecker, draws, like many of Nouri Al-Jarrah's poetic works, on diverse cultural sources. It is notable for its poignant interweaving of the historical and mythological heritage of the eastern Mediterranean with the present and past lives of Syrian families forced to escape the killings, war and destruction in their homeland in makeshift boats. The dramatic structure of this extraordinary poem enables the poet to reach back centuries as if it were just yesterday – so that the suffering Syrians give new voice to the Mediterranean's heroic past, as its ancients Sappho, Cadmus and Ulysses/Odysseus call out to them, 'gasping on dark shores', surrounded by emptiness, silence and rocks of pain. The call with the 'dying Syrians, trembling on the shores' being urged to 'Win the tumult of your souls', to go to the world and 'rise in every language and every book' . . . 'and surge in every territory'. With these metaphysical features and deep existential visions, the poet reveals the unique poetic voice that he has fine-tuned over time since he first attracted attention with his debut collection *The Boy*, published in Beirut in 1982.

A Boat to Lesbos and other poems also includes poems written while the poet visited Lesbos during the refugee crisis. The poems are complimented by illustrations of paintings by the Syrian artist Reem Yassouf. In addition to its original Arabic edition, the book has appeared in French, Italian, and Spanish editions, as well as the present English volume, which is the poet's first collection in English translation.

Nouri Al-Jarrah was born in Damascus in 1956. Since his debut collection of poems he has been an influential poetic voice on the Arab literary scene. He settled in London in 1986, publishing 14 further collections, and founding and editing a number of Arabic literary magazines. His poetry draws on diverse cultural sources, and is marked by a special focus on mythology, folk tales and legends. Selected poems have been translated into a number of Asian and European languages, and some collections have been published in French, Spanish and Farsi.

The two translators have a special interest in translating contemporary Arabic poetry. Camilo Gómez-Rivas is Associate Professor of Mediterranean Studies at the University of California, Santa Cruz, and Allison Blecker is a researcher associated with Swarthmore College, USA, with a PhD in Arabic Literature from Harvard University.

Margaret Obank, Banipal Books

لَوحٌ إغرِيقِيٌّ

(نِداءُ سافو)

I

أيُّها السُّوريُّونَ الأَليمُونَ، السُّوريُّونَ الوَسيمُونَ، السُّوريُّونَ
الاشِقّاءُ الهارِبُونَ مِنَ المَوتِ، أنْتُم لا تَصِلُونَ بالقَوارِبِ،
ولكِنَّكُم تُولَدُونَ عَلَى الشَّواطِئِ مَعَ الزَّبَدِ.
تِبْرٌ هَالكٌ أنتم، تِبْرٌ مَصْهُورٌ وَضَوءٌ مُصَوَّحٌ.
مِنْ لُجَّةٍ إلى لُجَّةٍ في خَاصِرةِ بَحْرِ الرُّوم، مَعْ نَجْمَةِ البَحْرِ
وشَقِيقِها الحَبّارِ التَّائِه، تُرسِلُكُم الأَمْواجُ في ضَوءِ بَنَاتِ نَعْشٍ.

20

Greek Tablet

(The Call of Sappho)

I

Suffering Syrians, beautiful Syrians, Syrian brothers
    fleeing death. You won't reach the shores on rafts
    but will be born on beaches with the foam.
Lost gold dust you are, melted gold dust, scattered,
    dulled.
From abyss to abyss in the hollow of the sea of the
    Rum, with the star fish and her brother, the roving
    squid, the waves convey you under the light of Ursa
    Major, the Daughters of Na'sh.

كَمَا تُولَدُ عَرَائِسُ البَحْرِ تُولَدُ الحَسْنَاوَاتُ السُّورِيَّاتُ، فِي ضَوْءٍ رَاجِفٍ وَيَطَأْنَ بِرَاحَاتِ أَقْدَامِهِنَّ الرَّخْصَةِ المُجَرَّحَةِ حَصَى لِسْبُوسَ وَرَمْلِهَا الرَّمَادِي..

انْزِلْنَ مِنْ فَاكِهَةِ الشَّامِ
إِلَى حِجَارَةِ الأَلَمِ.

أَيُّهَا السُّورِيُّونَ الأَشِقَّاءَ، السُّورِيُّونَ المُتَدَافِعُونَ مَعَ الْمَوْجِ، السُّورِيُّونَ المَقْتُولُونَ فِي الضِّفَافِ، المَحْمُومُونَ المُتَلَهِّفُونَ عَلَى السَّوَاحِلِ المُعْتِمَةِ بِوُجُوهٍ صَبِيحَةٍ، هُنَا، فِي لِسْبُوسَ الَّتِي طَالَمَا أَبْكَتْهَا طُرْوَادَةُ..

تَعَالُوا لِأَقْبَلَ خُدُودَكُمُ المُتَوَرِّدَةَ مِنَ الْجَزَعِ.

22

Like mermaids born in the quivering light, beautiful
    Syrian women set tender, wounded soles on the
    rocks and grey sand of Lesbos.

Come down from the fruits of al-Sham to the rocks
    of pain.

Brother Syrians, rolling on waves, killed on the
    beaches, feverish, gasping on dark shores with
    morning-like faces, here, in Lesbos that Troy made
    cry.

Come, let me kiss your cheeks, rosy with fear.

تَعَالَوا يَا أَحِبَّائِي، يَا مَنْ الْتَمَعَتْ فِي عُيُونِكِم رِمَالُ السَّوَاحِلِ، وَتَمَوَّجَ الشَّرْقُ فِي نُحَاسِ وُجُوهِكُم سَنَابِلَ ذَهَبٍ. اِنْهَضُوا كَمَا نَهَضَتْ فِي خَيَالَاتِ خُدُودِكُم الاسِيلَةُ جِبَالٌ عَالِيَةٌ، إِنَّكُم لَتَمِيشُونَ فِي خَيَالِي كَمَا مَاسَتْ فِي هَوَاءِ أَيَامِكُم أَشْجَارُ الْحُورِ وتَطَايَرَت أَزْهَارُ التُّفَاحِ فِي هُبُوبِ عُبُورِكُم. تَعَالَوا فِي عَتْمَةِ لِسْبُوس، أَيُّهَا السُّورِيُّونَ الْخَارِجُونَ مِنْ لَوْحِ الْابجديَّةِ الْمَكْشُوز.

اِنْزِلُوا وكُونُوا دَمَ الضَّوْءِ وحُرُوفَ اللُّغَةِ.

كَيْفَ، يَا طِفْلِي الصَّغِيرَ، لَمْ تَصِلْ إِلَى حُضْنِي، كَيْفَ رَدَّتْكَ الْمَوجَةُ عَنِّي وتَرَكَتْكَ هُنَاكَ عَلَى شَاطِئِ إِزْمِيرَ؛ مَلَاكاً بِلَا جَنَاحَينِ.

Come, friends. The sand of the shores gleaming in
your eyes, the East rippling golden ears of wheat in
the copper of your faces. Rise as the high
mountains rose in your smooth cheeks. You swing
in my mind as the poplars swung in the wind of
your days and the apple blossoms scattered in the
gale of your crossing. Come into the darkness of
Lesbos, you Syrians who emerged from the broken
tablet of the alphabet.

Come down, be the blood of light and the alphabet
of language.

How, my child, did you not make it into my arms?
How did the wave ebb away with you from me and
leave you there on the shore of Izmir, an angel
without wings?

أَجْوَدُ الخَمْرِ حَمَلْنَاهُ مِنَ اللّاذِقِيَّةِ فِي زِقَاقٍ؛ أَجْوَدُ الخَمْرِ؛ عِنَبٌ فِي قَوَارِبِ القَبَارِصَةِ، عَلَى أَكْتَافِ بَحَّارَةٍ مِنْ كِرِيتْ. عِنَبُ الشَّامِ، مِنْ دَارِيَّا، ودُومَا وَوَادِي الشَّامِيَاتِ عَلَى أَيدِيهِنَّ أَدْهَانٌ طَيِّبَةٌ.

أَرْسَلْتُ شَقِيقَاتِي الجَارَاتِ يَحْمِلْنَ المَاءَ، ذَهَبْنَ بِالمَاءِ العَذْبِ إِلَى الشَّاطِئِ، وَرَجَعْنَ بِصَبِيٍّ قُلْنَ إِنَّهُ نَائِمٌ، وَلَمَّا مَدَدْنَهُ فِي المِلَاءَةِ، رَأَيْنَاهُ بِلَا وَجْهٍ.

فِي الفَجْرِ قَلَّبَتْنِي أَفْكَارٌ كَانَتْ ضَوْءاً أَخْضَرَ وَضَوْءاً أَزْرَقَ؛ مَوْجَاتٌ بَارِدَةٌ حَمَلَتْ غَنَائِمَ وَأَسْلَاباً لِبَحَّارَةٍ وَمُسَافِرِينَ غَرِقُوا فِي بَحْرٍ بَعِيدْ.

We carried in skins the best wine from Lattakia. The
best wine. Grapes in the boats of Cypriots, on the
shoulders of sailors from Crete. Grapes from al-
Sham, from Darayya, Douma, and Wadi al-
Shamiyyat, sweet balm on their hands.

I sent my neighbouring sisters carrying water. They
took it to the beach and returned with a boy they
said was sleeping. When they laid him out on the
sheet we saw he had no face.

At dawn, I was turned inside out by thoughts of
green and blue light. Cold waves carried the spoils
of sailors and travelers drowned in a distant sea.

تَسْتَقْتِلُونَ عَلَى القَوَارِبِ، وَيَبْتَلِعُكُمُ البَحْرُ دُونَ
لِسْبُوسَ، وأَمُوتُ فِي صِقِلِّيَةَ هَارِبَةً مِنَ الْبَيتِ.
لَا تُصَدِّقُوا بُوسِيدُونَ، ولَا قَارِبَ عُولِيسَ.
لَا تُصَدِّقُوا الرَّسَائِلَ ولَا تُصَدِّقُوا الْكَلِمَاتِ.

لَمْ يَبْقَ مِنْ قُدْمُوسَ الهَارِبِ بِشَقِيقَتِهِ مِنْ صُوْرِ
الْمُخْتَرِقَةِ سِوَى حُطَامٍ فِي قَارِبٍ.

You fight for life on the boats, and the sea swallows
you before you land in Lesbos, while I die in Sicily
fleeing home. Don't believe Poseidon or Ulysses's
ship. Don't believe the letters and don't believe the
words.

Nothing is left of Cadmus fleeing with his sister from
Tyre in flames but shards on a boat.

صَوت

تُريدِينَني فِي لِبَاسِ الشَّهيدِ
وفِي مَاءِ صَمْتِكِ
مُسْتَلْقِيًا؛
مَشيئَتُكِ
أَنَّنِي
زَهْرَةٌ
فِي عُرْوَةِ الْقَميصْ.

Voice

You want me in the clothes of a martyr
stretched out
in the water of your silence.
It's your command
that I be
a flower
in the button hole of the shirt.

لَوْحْ

III

تَعَالَ نَمْشِي تَحْتَ سَمَاءٍ صَامِتَةٍ وَلها لِسَانٌ حَجَرِيٌّ
نَمْشِي عَلَى السَّنَوَاتِ.
نَمْشِي، نَمْشِي، وَنَتَمَرَّنْ،
نَمْشِي وَنُرْسِلُ الْكَلِمَاتِ مِنْ لِسَانٍ إِلَى لِسَانْ.
تَعَالَ نَفْتَحُ الْقَامُوسَ وَنُسَلِّمُ عَلَى الْكَلِمَاتِ،
نَفْتَحُ الصَّحَائِفَ وَنَقْرَأُ فِي الْوَرَقِ مَا كَتَبَ الشُّعَرَاءُ.
تَعَالَ نَمْشِي حُفَاةً عَلَى الصَّمْتِ، حُفَاةً، لِئَلَّا نَجْرَحَ الْكَلِمَاتْ.

32

Tablet

III

Let's walk under the silent sky whose tongue is stone
walk over the years
walk and walk and become habituated
walk and send words from tongue to tongue.
Let's open the dictionary and greet the words
Let's open the papers and read on their pages what
    the poets wrote.
Let's walk barefoot on this silence, so no word is
    wounded.

لِمَنْ هَذا الْقَميصُ بِياقَةٍ دامِيَةٍ
لِمَنْ هَذا الْمِعْطَفُ عَلَى الْمِشْجَبِ
يَقْطُرُ دَماً
وَهَذا الْأَثَرُ مِنْ خُطْوَةٍ عِنَدَ الْبابِ،
والرّائِحَةُ الغَريبَةُ في أُصُصِ الزَّهْرِ،
وَتِلْكَ الصَّيحَةُ الْمُعَلَّقَةُ في سَماءِ الْمَنْزِلِ،
لِمَنْ تِلْكَ الصَّيحَةُ؟

Whose shirt is this, with the bloody collar
Whose jacket is this, on the peg
dripping blood
this footprint at the door
and this strange smell in the flower pots
the scream suspended in the sky of the house
Whose scream is it?

سَأَمْشِي مَعَكَ وَأَمْشِي مَعِي
لِأَسْمَعَ خَطْوَتِي عَلَى رَصِيفِ الْبَحْرِ
خُطْوَةً فِي الظِّلِّ وَخُطْوَةً فِي النُّورِ الْجَرِيحِ؛
النُّورِ الْمُحَطَّمِ، النُّورِ الْمُمَزَّقِ عَلَى حَافَّةٍ
وَالَّذِينَ عَبَرُوا الْأَمْسَ أَشْبَاحٌ هَائِمَةٌ فِي نُورٍ مُحْتَرِقٌ.

I'll walk with you and with myself
hear my footsteps on the corniche
one step in the shadow and one in the injured light
the shattered light, frayed at the edges
those who crossed yesterday are ghosts wandering in
the burning light.

صَوتْ

أُتْرُكِ الشَّوكَ في الإِكْليلِ
وَالْخَشَبَ مُجَرَّحاً،
أُتْرُكِ الْكِتَّانَ مُبَلَّلاً
والشَّفَقَ حائِراً بِدَمِ الْمُسْتَلْقي.
صَوتُكَ في صَدَفَةِ،
ضوءٌ مُرسَلٌ مِنْ شُرْفَةِ الأَمسِ، وَالْوَرْدَةُ في لَيلٍ.
أُتْرُكْ لي حَصَى الشّاطِئِ،
وَانْدَفِعْ،
لِأَرَى الْبَحْرَ
مَوجَةً وَراءَ مَوجَةٍ،
وَالشِّراعَ عَلَى الْبَحرِ صَوتَ الْغَريقُ.

Voice

Leave the thorns on the crown
and the wood wounded
Leave the linen wet
and the twilight baffled by the blood of the one
    stretched out.
Your voice in a sea shell
a light emitted from the terrace of the past, the rose
    at night.
Leave me the pebbles of the beach
and push forward
so I can see the sea
wave after wave
the sail on the sea as the scream of the drowned.

لَوْحٌ إغْرِيقِيٌّ

(تلويحةُ سافو)

VIII

أَيُّهَا السُّورِيُّونَ الْهَلَاكِيُّونَ، السُّورِيُّونَ الْمُرْتَجِفُونَ عَلَى السَّوَاحِلِ،
السُّورِيُّونَ الْهَائِمُونَ فِي كُلِّ أَرْضٍ، لَا تَمْلَأُوا جُيُوبَكُم بِتُرَابٍ
مَيِّتٍ، أُهْجُرُوا الْأَرْضَ تِلْكَ وَلَا تَمُوتُوا. مُوتُوا فِي الْمَجَازِ،
وَلَا تَمُوتُوا فِي الْحَقِيقَة. أُتْرُكُوا اللُّغَةَ تَدْفِنْكُم فِي أَوْصَافِهَا،
وَلَا تَمُوتُوا وَتُدْفَنُوا فِي تُرَابٍ. لَيسَ لِلتُّرَابِ ذَاكِرَةٌ سِوى
الصَّمْتِ. أَبحِرُوا فِي كُلِّ جِهَةٍ، وَفُوزُوا بِضَجَّةِ أَرْوَاحِكُمْ.
وَوَرَاءَ الْعَاصِفَةِ والْهَشِيمِ انْهَضُوا فِي كُلِّ لُغَةٍ وَكُلِّ كِتَابٍ
وَكُلِّ أَجَلٍ وَكُلِّ خَيَالٍ، وَاَضطَرِبُوا فِي كُلِّ تُرَابٍ، وَاَنْهَضُوا كَمَا
يَنْهَضُ الْبَرْقُ فِي الْأَشْجَارِ.

لندن مابين صيف ٢٠١٥ وشتاء ٢٠١٦

Greek Tablet

(The Call of Sappho)

VIII

Dying Syrians, trembling on the shores. Syrians
   wandering across the earth. Don't fill your pockets
   with dead earth. Leave that earth and don't die.
   Die in metaphor not in reality. Let language bury
   you in its epithets. Don't die and be buried in
   earth. The earth has no memory, just silence. Set
   sail in all directions. Win the tumult of your souls.
   And after the storm and the damage, rise in every
   language and every book and every appointed time
   and every imagination and surge in every territory
   and rise like the lightning in the trees.

London, Summer 2015 – Winter 2016

FACTORY GIRLS

GIRLS

TAKAKO ARAI

EDITED BY
JEFFREY ANGLES

TRANSLATED BY
JEFFREY ANGLES, JEN CRAWFORD, CAROL HAYES,
RINA KIKUCHI, YOU NAKAI, & SAWAKO NAKAYASU

Factory Girls

by Takako Arai
Translated from the Japanese by Jeffrey Angles, Jen Crawford, Carol Hayes, Rina
Kikuchi, You Nakai & Sawako Nakayasu
Action Books; 2019

The first English-language volume from Japanese poet, performer, and publisher
Takako Arai, *Factory Girls*, is a collection of engaging, rhythmically intense
narrative poems set in a silk-weaving factory. Depicting the secretive yet bold
world of the women workers as well as the fate of these kinds of regional, feminine,
collaborative spaces in current-day Japan, this volume explores corporate and
climate catastrophes including the rise of Uniqlo and the 2011 earthquake, tsunami
and nuclear disaster. Poet-translator and critic Forrest Gander has described
Factory Girls as 'a book that no one forgets'.

Arai was born in 1966 in Kiryū, a city in central Japan known for textile
production. Her father managed a small, cottage-style weaving factory located on
the family property and, at its height, the factory employed a few dozen workers
– mostly women – to produce the high-quality, finely woven silks that the town
is known for. Many of Arai's poems focus on the lives of the women workers she
saw so intimately while growing up in and around her father's factory. Arai has
acknowledged that women have been traditionally associated with weaving for
centuries, but when Japan started its rapid modernization in the mid-nineteenth
century, the textile industry turned to women as its main source of cheap labor.
Women were also most immediately affected by the collapse of the textile industry
in the late twentieth and early twenty-first centuries.

In the poems 'When the Moon Rises' and 'Bobbins', Arai describes how textile
factories shaped women's lives, long after the factories had become decrepit. In
'Colored Glass', editor Jeffrey Angles writes, 'she imagines the ways that the factory
gets into the worker's soul in even more literal terms – this surreal poem describes
a girl swallowing a silkworm so that her body itself becomes the factory where
silk is produced'. Arai is consistently drawn to the personal, sexual lives of women
workers and the way their lives intersect with the factory.

Factory Girls was edited by Jeffrey Angles and co-translated by Jeffrey Angles,
Jen Crawford, Carol Hayes, Rina Kikuchi, You Nakai, and Sawako Nakayasu.
Arai also recognizes the importance of colloquial language, despite the fact that
standardized Japanese has been the dominant language for most modern and
contemporary poetry. Carol Hayes and Rina Kikuchi have characterized Arai's
poems in dialect as being composed of 'imagined language.' Angles explains,
'Within any particular dialect, there are significant individual variations between
speakers of different ages, social classes, and genders, thus making it necessary
for Arai to imagine and develop a particular style of speech for each narrator to
use. Needless to say, the specific textures and qualities of these dialectical choices

are difficult to reproduce in translation, especially considering that the most noticeable variations in English dialects come in pronunciation, which is difficult to represent on the page.' Seeing as how theatricality and voice are so important to Arai, it should come as no surprise to learn that she is a gifted performer. Of *Factory Girls*, poet Brandon Shimoda writes, 'Her poetry, through these brilliant translations, is, in fact, the kind of altar-as-homage-as-storytelling I need, especially now and always: that of the acute and deeply compassionate choreography of counting and recounting (sometimes into dancing) the dead.'

Johannes Göransson, Joyelle McSweeney, Paul Cunningham, and Katherine M. Hedeen, Action Books

月が昇ると、

だれもいない紡績工場の夜勤です
電球はひとつだけ、
ひとりでに糸車が回っていて
カシャン、というのは
ボビンがとり替えられる時の音です
ここが終いになって
もう十年たちますが、
月が昇ると、働きはじめるのです
珍しいオートメーション
戦後まもなく
機械に髪を巻き込まれ、
亡くなった女工さんがあったそうですが、
幽霊のしごとではありません
いえ、
漂うものもあるのですが、
工場にも、
癖がある、
こういうことです
癖というのは残りますから、
四十四年、糸繰りをしたばあさんは
今際の床でも
人さし指の先を舐めては撚り上げる、
そのしぐさから逃れることができません
冥土でも、そうでしょう
糸というのは限りなく細いですから
操るものたちの肉体に
かえって身ぶりが染み込んでしまうのです、
とり憑いてしまうのです
ほら、
女工さんの手先から
すうっと、
生糸を引き抜けば、
いつまでも踊っているではありませんか

When the Moon Rises

It is the night shift in an abandoned spinning factory
There is only a single light bulb here
The spools of thread turn by themselves
Click goes the bobbins
Changed by the machines
A decade has already gone by
Since this place shut down
But when the moon rises, it begins to work
Its strange automation
They say that soon after the war
A factory worker's hair got tangled
In the machines, killing her
There are things that float here
But this is not the work of ghosts
No
In the factory
There are peculiar habits
That is what I mean
Peculiar habits remain here
An old lady who spun thread
For forty-four years here
Still licks her index finger and twists
Even on her deathbed
She cannot escape the gesture
That must be true in the netherworld too
Since threads are so infinitely thin
Gestures sink into the bodies
Of those who manipulate the machines
And possess them
Look
How the raw silk thread
Is pulled smoothly
From the factory woman's fingers
Then dances endlessly

工場もそうです、
糸車の芯棒が
覚えてる、
鉄の粒子は
回りつづけていた向きに
もはや頭を垂れたままなのですから、
ガラン、
と乗りだします
月光がそそぐとき、
満ち干があるのは潮ばかりではないのです

ガラーン、
　　　　　ガラーン
糸車が回ってる、
糸たちが泳いでる、
だれもいない紡績工場

The factory is that way too
The axle of the spinning wheel
Remembers
The molecules of steel
Hang their heads in the
Direction in which they spin
Then get caught up
Clanging emptily
When the moonlight pours in
It is not just the tide that grows full

Emptily
       Emptily
The spinning wheels spin
The threads swim
Through the abandoned factory

ベットと織機

呼びだしが仕事だったんです、青リン坊のあたしの、
受話器おいて、工場サ駆けって
ジャンガンジャンガン、力織機が騒くなか、
耳もとへ背伸びして
「サッちゃん！　電話！」

あれは、ヤイちゃんへでありました
　　　　　　　　　　　紋切り場をツッ切って
　　　　　整経場をカッ切って
糸繰り場には、カレンダーのポルノ写真が、目ェ流しておりました
機械なおしの二人のほかは、みィんな女の工場に
銭湯のよう、
丸出しおっぱいは
こぼれます、ホンモンも
泣きじゃくれば、飲まサァなんねェ
赤ンぼオブって、通っておったんです、女工さんらは、
ベビーベットさ持ち込んで、稼ェでおったんです
機械油と髪油と乳臭さが、工場のにおい
吸いたかねェ、そんなモン
ベビーベットと力織機、ベビーベットに力織機、ベビーベットが力織機、
ジャンガンジャンガン、ジャンガンジャンガン

それは、ヤイちゃんへでありました
名うてさんでありました
真ッ赤な袈裟サ織りとげるには、
腕がえェ、眼がえェ、頭がえェ、あっこがえェ、
女のなかの女じゃなけりゃア　駄目なんです
いッつも言うヨ、おかみさんは
　　　　　　　　　　娘 知らずの坊さんバ
　　　　　　成仏さすンは、念仏じゃねェ

Beds and Looms

My job as an operator was to call them out
An inexperienced girl like me
Pick up the receiver, run to the factory floor
And among the noise of looms—*clackity-clack, clackity-clack*
Stand up straight and shout into the women's ears
'*Sat-chan, telephone!*'

The call that day was for Yai-chan
              I dashed through the places
        Where we punch the cards for the looms
Where we prepare the threads for the warp
Where we spin the thread, I saw a pornographic picture on the calendar
Like in a public path, breasts exposed
In a factory where all but the two loom fix-it men were women
They let the real thing spill over as well
When a baby cries, you've got to let them feed
The women working in the factory
Put their children on their back, carried them to the cribs
They saved their money
Machine oil, hair oil, and breast milk—
Those were the scents of the factory
I hated them, didn't want to breathe them in
Baby beds and power looms,
Baby beds plus power looms, baby beds as power looms
Clackity-clack, clackity-clack, clackity-clack, clackity-clack

The call was for Yai-chan
She had a reputation as a weaver
To finish weaving a bright red robe for a priest
You need good hands, good eyes, a good mind, a good vagina
It won't work if she doesn't, if she's not a woman among women
The woman manager would always say
                         Those priests never know women
                     It's not Buddhist recitations that let

　　　　　　　機織りゾ、
　　　　　　肌サ衣に摩ッつけるンが、慰さめゾ
ヤイの手は、冥土の川サ漕ぐ舟ヨ、大伽藍の僧正さまの
メーター四十万の金襴が、
支えておったんです
工場の生活を、
二十二人の工員さんの、その夫の焼酎代の、その姑の線香代の、
その息子の修学旅行の積立ての、

ヤイちゃんにもありました
店屋物のバイクの男とありました
在に、奥さん隠してて、
煮えくり返ッた腹ン中、伸びちまう　うどんのように
こと切れて、赤ンぼ　くれてまいました
で、なんです
三十路サ過ぎても、張りかえったままなんは、
一滴もらさず絞め上げたンですから、
ベビーベットと力織機、ベビーベットに力織機、ベビーベットが力織機の、
女工場のポルノ写真は、
一人だけ飲ます先ないヤイちゃんの、熟れたイコンでありました
　　　　　　　　　　　　　眉間バ皺さす、
　　　　　　　　心痛が、
　　　　　　夜なべ仕事サ　かッ立てるンゾ
　　　女の女　こさえるンゾ
えぇか、ヤイに手ェ合わせぇ
って、
おかみさんは　ひでぇネ

呼びだしでありました

一等奥におりました
せっかちが切ってしまうと、
掛けなおサにゃアなりません、工場のソロバンがあたしの速度です
駆けって、駆けって、

52

Them reach Nirvana
It's our woman weavers
It's the robes against their skin that calm their desires
Yai-chan's hand is the oar, rowing a small boat on the River of Three Hells
The gold-threaded brocade (four hundred thousand yen per meter)
Worn by the abbot of the high temple
Supported
The life of the factory
All twenty-two workers, their husband's liquor
Their mother-in-law's incense
Their sons' excursions at school

Yai-chan also had a child
With the delivery boy from the noodle shop
He kept his wife in the country a secret
Their relationship broke off, like noodles cooked to mush
In the stewing stomach of her anger
She gave the baby to her older sister and her husband
So that's why
Even though she was past thirty and her breasts were swollen
Not a single drop came out, nipples bound up tight
That's why the pornographic picture in the woman's factory by the
Baby beds and power looms, baby beds plus power looms, baby beds as power
   looms
Was an overripe icon of Yai-chan, she who had no one to give her milk
The woman manager would say,
                        'The worries that cause her to crease her brow
              Are what make her work late into the night
      Are what make her a woman among women
   We put our hands together and thank her'
Not a very considerate thing to say

My job was to call them out

Yai-chan was in the far back
If the caller got impatient and hung up
We had to pay to call them back so factory accounts determined my speed
I ran, I ran

　　　　　カッ蹴って、
ぎょうさん積まれた糸置き場に
平べったいモン、あるようでした
ジャンガンジャンガン動いてて、機械だけ
おらんのです、
機織り工場のマリア観音、おりません、立っとりません
寝ております、ベットです
　　ダブルベットば　担ぎ込んだヨ！
　　　　　　ヤイちゃんは、
　　　　　　　しておった！　お昼休みを、機械なおしの正やんと
ギギギギギィ——ッと
大腿骨の、

　　　　　　　　　　観音扉が

　　　　　　　　　　　　（ベビーはええが、ダブルはいかん、
　　　　　　　　　　と言えますか
　　　　　　　　腕サ拝む工場です
　　　　　　女のなかの女、
　　　　　のなかに　秘仏さんがオンならば、
　　開帳ならん、
と言えますか）

織り上がる、
ジャンガン、ジャンガン
本金の鳳凰どもが、
スダレのような鶏冠を響かせ、蹴爪を尖らせ
舞い上がる、
繻子の法衣の背模様に、袂模様に
剥きだし眼の雲龍が、髭たな引かす昇龍が、鱗ぬめらす妖龍が、
　　　　　　糸と、
　　　　　　糸の、
交わりつづける生産現場で
ダブルベットに
うごめくシーツの汗、吸ッつきに、

I ran as fast as I could
Where we stored the thread, piled with spools
I noticed something, something flat
Clackity-clack, clackity-clack, the machines were moving by themselves
She wasn't there
The Maria-Kannon of the Weaving Factory wasn't there
She wasn't standing there
She was asleep, she was in bed
She'd hauled in a double bed!
                    Yai-chan had been doing it
                    During the lunch breaks with Shō-yan who fixed the looms!
Femurs before her sacred gate
Must have *creeeeeeaked*
                    As they opened

                                        (Who can say a baby bed was acceptable
                                        But a double bed was not?
                                        The factory worshipped her skill
                              If in this woman among women
                    We had a secret buddha
          Who had the right to say
She shouldn't open her shrine?

Her loom weaves the robes
Clackity-clack, clackity-clack
Phoenixes in pure gold thread
                    Unfold line
                    By line
Combs falling forth like plumes, claws sharpening
Dancing up
In the patterns on the back and sleeves of the priest's satin robes
The open eyes of the cloud dragon, long whiskers of the rising dragon, scales
     covering the mystic dragon
Danced down
To the birthplace of the thread
Where they intertwined
With the thread
To breathe in the sweat of the rustling sheets

舞い下りる、
龍、鳳凰が、舌舐めずりする僧正さまが

ジャンガンジャンガン、ジャンガンジャンガン、
ダブルベットは力織機、ダブルベットで力織機、
　　　　　ダブルベットへ力織機、
おかみさんは
泡ふいて、
ご先祖さんの仏壇に　般若心経あげとりました

ジャンガンジャンガン、ジャンガンジャンガン、
色即是空、空即是色
^{シキソクゼークー　クーソクゼーシキ}

　　　　　呼びだしに、

　　　　　呼びだされ、

　　　　　女たちが呼びだされ、

From the double bed found there
Dragons, phoenixes, and lip-licking priests

Clackity-clack, clackity-clack, clackity-clack, clackity-clack
Double bed is a power loom, double bed as a power loom,
        double bed with a power loom
The woman manager
Foamed at the mouth in anger and
To this day still recites the Heart Sutra
Before the shrine of her ancestors

Clackity-clack, clackity-clack, clackity-clack, clackity-clack
Form itself is emptiness, Emptiness itself is form
Sex itself is emptiness, Emptiness itself is sex

        Call them out

        Be called out

        We women are called out

ヘルド

機械と女の喧騒が、夕ぐれへ吸い込まれても、
糸置き場におりました、あたしは
束に寄っかかると、首の痞(つか)えがおりました
鉱泉のにおいがします、絹が吐き出す夜気というのは、
幻燈です
ひとつだけ、電球が灯ってて
板戸の穴から覗く、工場のありようは、
幻燈です

冷たい指が
織り機のヘルドに触れようとしています
機の止まった夜にこそ、現れるのです、男は
経糸(たていと)の繁ぎ屋です
乾いたすきま風と、
フィラメントに、晃々としていくヘルドの、
ちいさな、ちいさな目の中へ
挿し込もうとしています、糸を
瞬(まばた)きのゆるされない
空ろの目、
機械とは
手というまえに
無数の、無名の、瞳の変身ですから、
糸の交差を、すみずみまで見届けるのは
そんな眼球たちですから、
ぶら下がるヘルドは、義眼と言ってもいいんです、女工さんの、
夜の男は
一本、一本
しらっと舐めあげ
突き通さねばなりません、
痛がるでしょう
男の背中も、あんなに震えていて、
眉をひそめたヘルドは
ほうり投げるでしょう、視線を、
格子窓の新月へ

The Healds

Clatter clatter—The looms and women fade into dusk
Here I am, still in the thread storeroom
Leaning on the spools of thread, the stiffness in my neck disappeared
A tang of sulphur, the night air the silk spits out
Is a magic lantern
Alone, a single bulb glows
Peering through the hole in the wooden door, the factory
Is a magic lantern

Cold fingers
To touch the healds of the loom
Just at night, when the looms are at rest, he appears, the man
The warp threader
To push the thread through
Into the healds, glittering in a draft of dry wind
Under the bulb's filament
Into their tiny, tiny eyes
Forbidden to blink
Vacant eyes
Because the looms
Before they are hands
Are numberless, nameless eyes
The kind of eyes
That watch every single threaded intersection
So the hanging healds are like the artificial eyes of the factory girls
The night man
Would push it through
First one, then the next
Lightly moistening each one with his tongue
It hurts
The man's back too trembles hard
Grimacing, the healds
Look away
Through the window grating towards the new moon

機械とは、
操つり人形かもしれませんね、織物工場では
通さなければ、はたらけないのです
通されれば、うごく瞳が持てるんです、ヘルドは
男へ
カタッと、
首の関節を折り
蒼い息を吹きかけます、その針に
滲む、
ルビーの血色こそ、視力です

一体、一体、吊るされて
天井から、
しのびこむ鎌いたちに
糸と、
糸が、
絡まると
ばんざいする、蹴り足する、
乗りだして組みあう肩、腹をかかえて開ける下顎
男は、
駆けよって、解そうとヤッキになりますが、
かまわれたいのさ
もっともっと、突ッ込んでよ
いかしてよ、
胸もとがはだけていくのは
手管です、マリオネットの女工たちの、
眼ざしが
月へもどれば
頬に、ツツッとつたいます、
男のこめかみから滴ってくる汗が

今ごろ、
生身の女工さんらは
家や寄宿や銭湯で、
　　　　湯浴みをしている、娘の寝顔を見てる、電話の受話器を
　　　　　　　　　　　　　　　おこうとしている
いいえ、
いいえ、

60

Are the looms
Marionettes perhaps? At this textile factory
If they don't let it in, they can't work
If they let it in, they get moving eyes, the healds
With a clack
Fold their necks
Towards the man
Releasing pale breath, along the needle
A spreading blur
This ruby-red blood gives them sight

Hung up, one beside the other
From the ceiling,
The sneaking whirlwinds catch
This thread
Then that
All entangled
Arms lift—*banzai!*—legs kicking
Leaning forwards, embracing shoulders, holding bellies, laughing jaws
The man
Races over, desperate to untangle them
Each demanding more attention
More, more, penetrate me
Make me come!
Slyly exposing their breasts
The feminine wiles   of the marionette factory girls
When their coaxing gaze
Returns to the moon
Sweat drips from the man's temples
Running down both cheeks

Right about now
The real flesh and blood bodies of the factory girls
Take their baths at home, boarding houses, and public baths
        Or watch the sleeping faces of their daughters or move to hang up
                                        their phones
No
No

梳しけずる
ゆたかな髪が、風にもつれる、
十一時かっきりに
挿し入れようとするはずです、櫛を
鏡にうつして、

乗り出して組みあう肩、腹をかかえて笑う下顎
糸まみれの人形です、
ヘルドは
いいえ、あたしたちは
操られて、操らして、操つって、
男がビームを回せば、
攣りあがります、
生えぎわが、毛穴ごと、
なんと気持ちの佳いことでしょう
丹念に
一条、一条、束ねては、
巻き上げます、男は
色とりどりのすじ糸を、あたしたちの毛髪を、
なんと艶めくことでしょう

夜の工場に、夜の女工と、夜の髪結いさん
幻燈です
たったひとつの白熱球が、
振り子のように
揺すられて
サッと、
消える
繋ぎ屋といっしょに、
牛乳瓶を配達する、バイクの音がひびく前に

朝の光は、
人形を
機械に見してしまうでしょうが、
知ってるよ
男が置いてくつげ櫛を、

女工なら、

Combing their locks
Their rich hair, tangles in the wind
At precisely eleven o'clock
Forcing it through their hair, the comb
Is reflected in the mirror

Leaning forwards, embracing shoulders, holding bellies, laughing jaws
The marionettes are tangled in threads
The healds are
No, we are
Being manipulated, allowing ourselves to be manipulated, manipulating him to
    manipulate us
As the man rolls up the warp beam
All are pulled up
The roots of our hair, each and every hair follicle
How good it feels!
Delicately
First one strand, then the next, weave together
Hoisting them up, the man works on
The multicoloured threads, our hair,
How alluring we look!

The night factory, the night factory girls, the night coiffeur
All of them, a magic lantern
The single light bulb
Like a pendulum
Swinging
Suddenly
Vanishes
With the warp threader
Before the echoes of the milkman's motor bike

The morning light
Makes the marionettes
Look like looms
But you know
All about the wooden comb the man leaves behind

If you're a factory girl, that is

翳たち

ぐァらッと、崩されちまった場所で、
区別がつかない
ゴミと、
ゴミでないもの、まだ使っていけるものへも
土砂ぼこりが
あんまりも降りつもり、
見渡すかぎりゴミ箱なのだ
袖口で拭いた鼻水が、黒い
喉も肺も、浸蝕されて、
もうこのままでいい……放心を、
ナケナシが
ふり絞って、たくし上げても、

更地にしてはいけンのです
こうなる前に落としたビー玉を
拾うまでは、
せめて行李ひとつ分、
屑の中から、生ッ粋のガラクタを択るまでは、

一切、剥ぎとられンです、
消えるンです、
手を伸ばし、引きとどめねばなりません
きっと開けることない柳行李に
この土地の翳たちを、

64

Shadows

In this place suddenly thrown into disarray
It is impossible to distinguish
Between what is garbage
What is not and what is still useable
So much earth, sand and dust
Has fallen that
Everywhere I see
A great can of refuse
The mucus I wipe on my sleeve is black
My throat and lungs are eroded
Let it be, just the way it is…
Listless and resigned, I roll up my sleeves
And muster what little enthusiasm I can

I can't let this be turned into a vacant lot
At least until I pick up the marble
I dropped here before things got this way
At least until I pick through the refuse
And save at least one suitcase's worth of pure junk

This place will be completely stripped away
This place will disappear
I must stretch out my hands
And hold fast to
The shadows of this land
Even if only in a suitcase I will surely
Never open again

ねんねんころりよ

神秘でありました、おがむのが
日課でありました、朝の
しんぶんで、
びちゃびちゃと　愛液たたえる大釜へ
口しめ抜いた男茎が、ムンずと
つッこみ、掻きまわし、
いいえ、
スポーツ紙の文芸欄ではありません
かざられたではありませんか
あの日から、第一面に
その図解_{イコン}は、

化ケモノでありました、淫ヨクの
火ばしらの、燃料ボーが
原シ炉という子宮　の中で、
もてあましておりました、ゼツリンを
びちゃびちゃびちゃびちゃ
とけて、漏れてもおりました、っけ

ずいぶん　忘れちゃったよね
喰われてるんじゃありませんか
のうミソは、電脳_{パソコン}に、
アッチのほうは

原発に、けっきょくお盛んですぞ
赤んぼうの半減期に
わーんと生まれる、デン子たち
ねんねん、ころりよ

Come, Come, Fall Fast Asleep

It was a mystery, praying
Became our daily ritual, in the morning
Newspapers,
A male member, slushy, sloshing,
Trying to hold back, presses hard into a grand pot,
Wet with a woman's arousal, and stirs
No
I'm not talking
About the erotic stories in some men's paper
Ever since that day, wasn't that the icon
That adorned the front pages of our news?

It was a monster,
A fiery pillar of lust, the fuel rod
In the uterus of the nuclear reactor
It had lost control, a real stud
Slushy, sloshing, stewing, brooding
Melting and dripping out, whoa!

We had pretty much forgotten
The electric brains of our computers
Had eaten into our brains
That thing down there

Still the nuclear plant keeps doing it
In the mere half-life of an infant
Bunches more electric children are born with a wail
While we sing the lullaby
Come, come, fall fast asleep

in versions by
Anthony Howell

Incomprehensible Lesson

Fawzi Karim

CARCANET

Incomprehensible Lesson

by Fawzi Karim
In versions by Anthony Howell after translations from the Arabic made by the author
Carcanet; 2019

The death of Fawzi Karim in May 2019 was a great sadness but not a shock to Carcanet. He had been ill for quite a spell. He was therefore urgently concerned that his work exist as eloquently and accurately as possible in English even though, as he had told Tara Bergin, 'I do not *live* among English people […] I do not have English friends.' He remained, inevitably, haunted by Iraq, its landscape, people, and the horrors he had witnessed there. The American composer Michael Hersch, who worked with him and set his lines to music, noted his eyes, and how they expressed anguish and restraint, an urgency calmed. For him, the energy of the simple, truthful sentence delivered, without adjectival inflation, the greatest beauty or the bleakest truth.

When he died, Jenny Lewis, the poet and translator of *Gilgamesh*, paid him a tribute. Like me, she did not know him well personally, only met him once. Her tribute begins with a response to the collaborative translations of his work by Anthony Howell who, in *Incomprehensible Lesson*, worked with the poet himself: Fawzi producing the literals and talking Anthony through them. Jenny speaks of the English versions as 'wonderfully vibrant'. She also acknowledged the 'huge sadness and a sense of incomparable loss within the literary Arab world at his passing'. He played a significant part in the diaspora, not least in becoming genuinely audible in the host language.

Hersch's collaboration resulted in significant musical works. 'He was both a friend and a tremendous inspiration. His best work has a concision which goes to the heart of any matter, often uncomfortable to many. The work is without excess or a heavy hand, without surface-level regret or sentimentality.' He added, 'When I think of Karim, the words of the American sculptor Christopher Cairns come to mind. Cairns once said while discussing his own work that, amongst other motivations, he attempts to convey *love… the love of humankind, even in its catastrophic relationship to where it is going.* Or, in Karim's case, where humankind had been as well.'

Hersch met Karim at the home of another expatriate, this time a Canadian through whom I also made Fawzi's acquaintance, the poet and essayist – in the widest, most humane sense – Marius Kociejowski. In 2009, Kociejowski contributed a major essay on Fawzi, his life and work, to *PN Review*. It was this essay, entitled 'Swimming in the Tigris, Greenford: The Poetical Journey of Fawzi Karim', that fired my curiosity and eventually my editorial commitment to the poet. Many poets owe Kociejowski a debt of gratitude. I can say that Carcanet would have been a different publishing house without his patient advocacies and without his own considerable work as a poet and prose writer.

In correspondence with me, Fawzi was keen on getting things right: the relationship of the poet to the translator, how this should be expressed, how the poems should look, what impact the cover should have. He was clear what he wanted and got his way much of the time. I did not know him as Marius or Michael did, or as Anthony Howell who worked so closely with him – I can imagine the warmth and tension in that relationship! – but got to know the poems. When he sent work for *PN Review* I would turn back some of the poems because I was not persuaded; others were spot on and stood, and stand, almost as though they had been conceived in English. He did have English (or in any case Canadian and American) friends. They understood him as well as, maybe better than, some of those who read his poems in the original. There are advantages in working at one remove, at bringing two cultures into tentative, suggestive intimacy by accommodating them in another language and finding them a readership in it. This is why the Sarah Maguire Prize is so important: it is a way of turning up the volume of the news that stays news, of alerting listeners to the dissonance and harmony of voices that are the single voice emerging from a translation. Reviewing Fawzi's poems in *Berfrois*, Jessica Sequeira wrote, 'These are poems of the self, a turn toward not just the past but the deep past, the past of myth.'

Michael Schmidt, Carcanet

لأنه يحدُثُ كلَّ يوم

لأنه يحدثُ كلَّ يوم
من دونِ أن يُعلنَ عن ساعته.

يحدثُ فجأةً، كما يومِضُ نيزكٌ
على بشَرةِ الليلِ المجعّدة.

أو أنه يتركُ عن درايةٍ لحظَتنا مُهدّدة
بعبءٍ ماضينا، ولا يسكُنُنا، ويمضي.

لأنه يَبغَتُنا،
كقطرةٍ مُفاجئة
من دمِنا،
تبلُّ، حين نبدأ الكتابةَ، الورقَ.

وبالعرقِ
يبتلُّ من لسانِه الصمغي
لباسنا التحتي.

لسنا ضحاياه، ولكنّنا
محضُ أدلةٍ على حضوره.

72

Because It Happens Every Day

Because it happens every day
Without announcing its time,

Happens suddenly, just as a comet
Flashes on the night's wrinkled skin,

Or leaves our very moments under threat
Of collapse beneath the weight of our past,

Because it comes and goes,
Because it startles us

With its sudden drop in pressure,
The paper sweats as we start writing.

A sticky tongue
Has left our underwear damp.

We are not its victims but
Its evidence.

Central Line

على مقربة من بيتي في Greenford
تتوقف عرباتُ الCentral line
لحظاتٍ، ثم تولي تقطع لندن نصفينْ

تأخذني، حين تلحّ عليّ الاسئلةُ: إلى أينْ؟،
لشوارعَ ومبانٍ وحدائقَ أفسدَها التكرارْ،
أتصيّدُ بين مراياها النسخَ الحائلةَ اللون لوجهي،

ثم أعودُ بذات «الخطِّ الأحمرِ» للدازْ.
من إطلالة Waterloo يُدهشني
أن كمالَ المشهد سرعانْ

ما يبدو لي لوحةَ فوتوغراف بإطازْ،
والحشدَ السائحَ، إذْ تتبعثر فيه الألوانْ
كوليمةِ عرس، يبدو لي عرضاً في شاشة تلفاز.

وإذا ما اقتحمتْ كلَّ محاذيري
سيدةٌ في حفل، أتلبّس دورَ المنفي
عن غير إرادة.

وإذا ما انتصفَ الليلُ
واسترختْ قدّامي فوق المقعد
سنواتُ العزلة والتيه،
أخرجتُ جوازَ السفر
وقضينا الليلَ نحدّقُ فيه.

Central Line

Close to my home in Greenford,
The carriages roll to a halt. After long moments
They go on to bisect London.

The line takes me (questions harass) 'Where?'
To streets, buildings, parks marred by repetition,
So that I prefer my own blurred reflection.

Then I return by the same red line,
Musing how, from Waterloo Bridge,
The scene's perfection amazed me:

Seemed an artistic print, framed in an exhibition,
How the tourists milling there
Scattered such colours – like a wedding breakfast –

Was it some performance on TV?
A lady at a party broke through my precautions.
I found myself once more in the role of exile.

The line goes on and on. The years
Sit across from me. I take out my passport.
They want to share its pages.

المدينة المنسية

لعلة ما هجرت أعشاشها الطيور .
المطر الساقط والبيوت في الأصيل
مشاهدٌ قد ظُللتُ بقلم رصاص.
والريح بالسياط قد جمّدت اللسان
وسط ركام الخرق الرثة والجرائد.

لعلة ما هجرت أعشاشها الطيور .
لعلة، هجرتَ انت الآخر البيت ولم
تترك سوى آثار أقدامك.
كنتَ تعيد النظر الفاحص في الأمواج.

آثار أقدام... وأوراق على الأرصفة
وفورة الشمس على معصم هذه المدينة
صارت سوار فضة بارد.
زانت به معصمها
صبية من زمن بائد.

The Forgotten City

Late afternoon. The houses shaded.
No, it's pencil strokes of rain.
The birds have flown, their nests abandoned.
The wind applies its whips,
While the tongue freezes amid
Rags and tatters of newsprint.

The birds have flown, their nests abandoned.
And you too, you out-of-place Tuareg,
You've left nothing but footprints.
Come to the waves too late,
    you've stared at them too long.

Echoes of footfalls… leaves in a whirl…
Once a scorcher burnt the wrist of this metropolis.
Now it has cooled to a bracelet of silver
Worn just the once, an age ago, by some forgetful girl.

مشهد، وصوت مُنشدين

الإله الذي كنتُ أنكرتُه دخلَ البيت.
في البيتِ كان أبي ساعةَ النزعِ.
أمي وأبناؤها، يتحاشونَ رؤيتَه
راقداً في البياض.
وأنا، بينهم، أتحاشى الحضورَ الجليل
للإله الذي كنتُ أنكرتُه.

كان سمحَ الجبين، يفيضُ عليه الرداءُ،
وفي مقلتيهِ ابتلالٌ، وفي طرفِ الشفتينِ ابتسامةُ إشفاق.
يتحاشى النظر
في الوجوه التي أعتمتْ،
وهي ترقبُ كيف سيكشف عن هوّةٍ جسدٌ راقدٌ في البياض.

«نحنُ نُصغي،
وليس لنا غيرُ حق ابتهالْ
للإلهِ.
وفي الفم، مما نراهُ،
مرارةُ حقِّ السؤالْ
الذي لا يحقّ لنا!»

كان حزني رهينَ المسرّة في جسدي،
والمسرةُ إسراءَ حزني إلى الغيب!

تأملتُ فيه انحناءةَ شيخ أضر به الدهرُ،
هيكلَ صرح تصاغرَ حتى اغتدى ملجأً خرباً
للذي لا ملاذ له.
كان يحتاطُ من أنْ يُرى وهو يرحلُ.
أحتاطُ من أنْ أُرى وأنا في اقتفاء خطاه.
فتحَ البابَ سرّاً، وسرّاً طويتُ الطريقَ الى مُنتهاه.

78

Seeing and Pleading

My father, now in white, undergoes his agonies,
And the god I have always denied enters the house.
My mother, sisters, brother, in a half-circle there,
Haven't noticed, haven't raised their eyes.
I am the only one to have seen him coming in.
And I'm the only one who is trying not to look at him.

The god is crying, this god I have always denied,
For isn't he full of his always infinite pity?
The shadow of death hangs over the family.
Soon there'll be nothing but darkness.
An emptiness will engulf my father's body.

There is a listening though.
Our sole right is to plead.
We cannot ask the question which is always on our lips,
Aching to be spoken.
From frustration such as this bitterness must flow.

But here is the god, hunched over, blasted by time,
A ruined place, sole refuge now
For refugees from who knows where.
He slips away, so quietly,
But, doggedly, unseen, I follow after,

Both of us lost, in the way some stars get lost,
Through desert dust, and mirages
Of water which recede from us forever
Like travellers who went before...
Their bones repeat the moaning of the wind
Across these wind-lashed spaces, the wolves not far behind.

معنا حيرةُ النجمِ، غبراءُ كلَّ صحارى العرب،
وماءُ السرابِ.
معنا هالةُ الراحلين
قبلنا.
معنا من عظامٍ هياكلِهم ما يُقيتُ الرياحَ،
ويُبْقي صدىً لعواءِ الذئابِ.

«نحنُ نُصغي،
وليس لنا غيرُ حق ابتهالْ
للإلهِ.
وفي الفمِ، مما نراهُ،
مرارةُ حقٍّ السؤالْ
الذي لا يحقّ لنا!»

There is a listening though.
Our sole right is to plead.
We cannot ask the question which is always on our lips,
Aching to be spoken.
From frustration such as ours bitterness must flow.

الحكاية

حفنةٌ من زهور البنفسجِ، بعثرَتُها فوق فَوَّهةِ البئرِ،
لمْ تغِبِ الشمسُ، لكنَّ زهرَ البنفسج سرعانَ ما فقدَ اللونَ
حينَ تبعثرَ، سرعانَ ما فقد الرائحة.

كنتُ ألهو، وأجهلُ أن البنفسجَ لا يُحسنُ اللهوَ.
واليومَ أعرفُ أن الحكايةَ، وهي تعودُ ليوم الصبا، ذاتُ مغزى
يحاوزني بأسى العارفين.

فزهرُ البنفسج يُشبه في فرطِ رقّته الكلمة،
إذ أحاولُها عابثاً وهي في عزِّ فطرتِها،
تَتَهاوى ببئرِ المعاني وتُعتمُ،
تُمسي، على غير ما أشتهي، كالمجسَّةِ
تبحثُ في البئر عَمّا التأمَ
من جراح فَتَفْتقُّها.
فإذا بي أرى البئرَ أرملةً باكية.

كيف يحدثُ هذا معَ الكلمة؟
كلما جئتُ أسعى لبستانها كنتُ عن لا إرادة
معطفاً يترنّح تحت المطر؟

هي ظلُّ الذي لا يُرى في رواق العبادة،
هي راعية العزلة المستعادة
حين أكتب.

The Tale

There was a bunch of violets I let fall
Into the depths of a well.
The sun still gleamed on them, but they soon
Lost their colour, then they lost their smell.

And so I played with time, not realising
That the violets would not be amused.
And today, I know this story has to do with my boyhood
And days which speak to me sadly, knowingly too.

Each petal seems like some word that's especially tender,
And what was I doing? Just having fun with its innocence,
Letting it fall, letting it fall into a well of meaning
Only to grow confused.

The word becomes like an instrument
Probing a wound on the mend simply to breach it again.
And then I see in the well a widow's tears.
How is it all this appears – out of a word?

With its garden in sight, I can't help but become
A coat beaten back by the rain.
It's the shadow of the unseen in the arbour,
Isolation's patron, always stooping over what I write.

الدرس العصي

في ساعةِ المغيبِ تبدو سحبُ الخريف
مثل قطيعِ ماشية
منثورةٍ خِرافُه على المدى المُطلقِ.
ستةُ سيقانٍ لنا في فتحةِ التنورْ
ونحنُ حولَها جلوسٌ، نأكلُ الخبزَ،
ونُحصي في المدى المنظورْ
أيامَنا الهانئةَ التي تبقّتْ،
قبل أن نباشرَ العامَ الدراسي.

تُقبلُ أمي كلَّ حين لترى ملاكَها الحارس
يحيطُنا بالدفءِ والرعاية.
تُصغي إلى رسائلِ الطيورِ في القافلةِ المهاجرة
لها، لكلِّ كائن منتظرٍ يُشبهها،
ثانيةً، وتمضي.
كأنها تُلقّنُ الدرسَ العصيَّ لي، أنا الشاعرْ
في مقتبلِ العمر.

لذا يرفعني التنهّدُ الخفيُّ دون أخوتي،
أعلى من النخيلْ.
ثم أعودُ فاقدَ الدفءِ لدفءِ إخوتي الجميلْ.

وفجأةً يخطِفني الطائرُ ذو المخالبِ الكاسرة،
يعبُرُ بي العمرَ، الذي يُشبه في احتراسه
مدينةً محاصرة.
وإذ تحينُ غفلةٌ من الزمان
يقذِفُني حول رَحى الحاضر.

84

Incomprehensible Lesson

At the hour of sunset, autumn clouds
    are scattered sheep drifting towards the distance.
The six stalks of our feet dangle over the lip
    of the clay oven.
We hang around like that, eat warm bread,
    while counting the sheep of the days we have left:
Happy days that remain before we're packed off to school.

My mother comes to shepherd us from time to time.
I listen to the birds,
    and to what they want me to report to her
    as they pass in their migratory convoys.
The message is for anybody waiting,
    waiting like her, while the birds are here
    for a little while, and then they're off on their way again.
It is as if this is teaching me some incomprehensible lesson.
Already I'm a poet in my prime.

It is thus that a hidden sigh
    lifts me above my brothers,
Higher than the palm tree,
And then I'm back, cold from the heights,
Back within their captivating warm.

All too soon, the sharp-clawed hawk will snatch me,
The hawk that hovers over my life,
A life, which in its vigilance
    resembles a city under siege.
And only in the negligence of time
    can the hawk stoop, drop onto me
The present moment, heavy as a millstone.

وها أنا أدوز
دورتَها، بلا طحينٍ،
ثم لا أنفكُّ أُحصي في المدى المنظور
ما أبقت الأيامُ، قبلَ أن أباشرَ الدرسَ العصيّ!

And here I am, ground round and round as it turns,
grinding no flour whatsoever.
I can't help counting the days that are left
And what the days have in store
Before I have to revise that incomprehensible lesson.

HYSTERIA

Kim Yideum

Translated by
Jake Levine, Soeun Seo, Hedgie Choi

Hysteria

by Kim Yideum
Translated from the Korean by Jake Levine, Soeun Seo and Hedgie Choi
Action Books; 2019

Born in Jinju in 1969, Kim Yideum is a South Korean poet and the author of seven collections of poetry. Following Action Books' publication of her 2015 English language debut, *Cheer Up, Femme Fatale*, Kim's second collection, *Hysteria*, continues to evoke the grotesqueries of her first work, while simultaneously delving further into the materiality of everyday life. Through an overflowing that echoes fellow feminist poet Kim Hyesoon, and a blunt, down-to-earth language that is unique to the poems, Hysteria rides through the surface of wage labor, patriarchy, and subsistence, proceeding through a variety of personas, human and otherwise, along an intensity that demands to be seen as it is, to be taken at face value. Kim Hyesoon has described Kim Yideum's work as a 'landscape of confession', noting how 'confession flows inside the landscape and the landscape soars inside the confession'.

Kim's poems are known for their grotesque and provocative motifs. Disrupting and resisting established Korean literary traditions, her characters often possess multiple personalities. The poems of Hysteria feature night travellers, teachers, mothers, queers, prostitutes, nauseating fathers, and nauseated women. Vengeful and destructive, Kim's voice never stops expanding to condemn and conquer shame. Her poetry reimagines the rules of society and sides with its victims.

Hysteria was translated by Jake Levine, Soeun Seo, and Hedgie Choi. In his translator's note, Levine notes that 'Translation always starts as collaboration' and compares the experience of translating Kim to the multiplied self in the paintings of Chun Kyung-Ja. 'While there might be multiple characters and/or speakers, each speaker offers an additional personality to an expanding and multitudinous self. That sense of 'self' is a performance. Reality is always on-stage'. At times, Kim's revolving cast of speakers made identifying speakers a challenge for Levine. The translators also faced the dilemma of translating Korean puns into English. 'Instead of translating literally, we had to read into the affect. Luckily, we had editors who kept reminding us that good translation is interpretive and creative', writes Levine.

Soeun Seo began translating Kim Yideum in the summer of 2015 and ended in the summer of 2018. They and Hedgie Choi have cited Kim's aggressive style as a source for inspiration. Observing a unique 'irritability', Seo claims to have actively channeled their own anger before translating the poems of *Hysteria*. This choice to translate from a place of rage led to some inventive and radical translation choices. 'I remember thinking, oh, what if this translation is too loose and Jake and Hedgie don't like it, but the reactions were really good, and I felt very validated in that method of translating', says Seo. Hedgie Choi has described the collaborative translation process as 'freeing', expressing much appreciation for Levine and Seo's willingness to give suggestions and overall receptiveness. 'When any of us tried to be free, we all tried to validate each other, and we were very supportive about it', says Seo.

In October 2020, *Hysteria* was named both the National Translation Award winner as well as the Lucien Stryk Asian Translation Award winner, by The American Literary Translators Association, the first time any title has received both prizes.

Johannes Göransson, Joyelle McSweeney, Paul Cunningham,
and Katherine M. Hedeen, Action Books

사과 없어요

아 어쩐다, 다른 게 나왔으니, 주문한 음식보다 비싼 게 나왔으니, 아 어쩐다, 짜장면 시켰는데 삼선짜장면이 나왔으니, 이봐요, 그냥 짜장면 시켰는데요, 아뇨, 손님이 삼선짜장면이라고 말했잖아요, 아 어쩐다, 주인을 불러 바꿔달라고 할까, 아 어쩐다, 그러면 이 종업원이 꾸지람 듣겠지, 어쩌면 급료에서 삼선짜장면 값만큼 깎이겠지, 급기야 쫓겨날지도 몰라, 아아 어쩐다, 미안하다고 하면 이대로 먹을 텐데, 단무지도 갖다 주지 않고, 아아 사과하면 괜찮다고 할 텐데, 아아 미안하다 말해서 용서받기는커녕 몽땅 뒤집어쓴 적 있는 나로서는, 아아, 아아, 싸우기 귀찮아서 잘못했다고 말하고는 제거되고 추방된 나로서는, 아아 어쩐다, 쟤 입장을 모르는 바 아니고, 그래 내가 잘못 발음했을지 몰라, 아아 어쩐다, 전복도 다진 야채도 싫은데

No Apology

Shit. What's this expensive dish? I didn't order this. I said
jjajangmyeon, you know, simple noodles with black bean sauce?
Look, here. *No, Ma'am. You said seafood.* Really? Should I get
the owner? Make him fix it? Shit. If I complain this dude
will get bitched at. The price will be deducted from his wage.
Or worse, he'll get the axe. I'd eat it if he apologized, but he
didn't give me pickled radishes. He didn't say sorry. If only
he had apologized. To me who doesn't receive forgiveness,
to me who takes the blame. Me expelled, me deleted, after
not putting forth the effort to argue, why is it always me who
apologizes? It's not like I haven't been in his shoes, but maybe I
mispronounced the dish? Shit. I'm really gonna eat it. Even
though I hate abalone. Fuck sliced vegetables.

피의 10일간

그 섬에 가서 돼지를 잡자
우물가에서 돼지 잡아
넘쳐흐르는 내장까지 나눠 먹자 했죠
천일염도 한 포대씩 받아 오자 했죠

그 친구 죽고 나면 그 돼지 누가 잡아 따뜻한 콩
팥을 나눠줄까요
하늘 높이 올라가는 방광을 주세요

당신은 번역하고 해석하느라 약속을 잊으셨지요

얘기해주세요
그날이 어땠는지
누가 어떻게 종지부를 찍었는지
백범도 육당도 몰라요
당신이 말해줘요 직접 본 사람들은 입을 다물고
늙어 죽어갑니다

나는 요즘 애
영어가 급하죠 참는 건 아니에요
재떨이가 담뱃불을
도마가 칼을 견딘다 비약하지 마세요

이 날짜에 비상해지죠
가장 민감하게 반응하는데 필요 없는 물건도 훔치
고 싶어요
팬티 내리고 생리대를 똑바로 놓지만
뛰어다니는 날엔 이게 다 무슨 소용인가 싶어요

Ten Days of Blood

Let's go to that island and catch a pig!
You said, *Over by the well, let's catch the pig. Split*
the pig. Eat its overflowing guts! You said
Let's grab a bag of salt.

Who will catch the pig after my friend is dead?
Who will I share the warm kidneys with?
Give me the bladder flying high to heaven!

Did you forget our promise
because you were busy translating, analyzing?

Tell me
how was that time of the month?
Where in that sentence did you put the period?
Not even Kim Koo or Yukdang knew how to do it.
Tell me! Those that saw it kept their mouths shut.
They grew old and died.

Lately I'm a baby.
I need English desperately and I'm not resisting.
Don't assume that the ashtray will survive the cigarette's flame
that the cutting board can endure the knife.

Today is a date that has become extraordinary.
Hypersensitive, I want to steal shit I don't need.
I pull my panties down and put the pad on straight
but running around all day, I think to myself
what's the point?

피의 일주일이 지나면 피임 날짜나 세는 요새 젊
은것들이라서

당신은 고향에 내려졌던 비상계엄령에 관해 우물
과 시장에 관해 말하지 않나요

나는 보챕니다

불타는 파출소 옆에서
자궁을 꺼내 하늘 높이 차올리고 싶은 날이니까요

You are the kind of person
who doesn't talk about what happened at the well and in the market
the day your hometown fell into martial law
and I'm like the so-called youth
I count my birth control pills and bitch about everything.

Next to the burning police station
I want to tear out my uterus and kick it to heaven.

히스테리아

이 인간을 물어뜯고 싶다 달리는 지하철 안에서
널 물어뜯어 죽일 수 있다면 야 어딜 만져 야야 손
저리 치워 곧 나는 찢어진다 찢어질 것 같다 발작하
며 울부짖으려다 손으로 아랫배를 꽉 누른다 심호흡
한다 만지지 마 제발 기대지 말라고 신경질 나게 왜
이래 팽팽해진 가죽을 찢고 여우든 늑대든 튀어나오
려고 한다 피가 흐르는데 핏자국이 달무리처럼 푸른
시트로 번져가는데 본능이라니 보름달 때문이라니
조용히 해라 진리를 말하는 자여 진리를 알거든 너
만 알고 있어라 더러운 인간들의 복음 주기적인 출
혈과 복통 나는 멈추지 않는데 복잡해죽겠는데 안
으로 안으로 들어오려는 인간들 나는 말이야 인사
이더잖아 아웃사이더가 아냐 넌 자면서도 중얼거리
네 갑작스런 출혈인데 피 흐르는데 반복적으로 열렸
다 닫혔다 하는 큰 문이 달린 세계 이동하다 반복적
으로 멈추는 바퀴 바뀌지 않는 노선 벗어나야 하는
데 나가야 하는데 대형 생리대가 필요해요 곯아떨어
진 이 인간을 어떻게 하나 내 외투 안으로 손을 넣
고 갈겨쓴 편지를 읽듯 잠꼬대까지 하는 이 죽일 놈
을 한 방 갈기고 싶은데 이놈의 애인을 어떻게 하나
덥석 목덜미를 물고 뛰어내릴 수 있다면 갈기를 휘
날리며 한밤의 철도 위를 내달릴 수 있다면 달이 뜬
붉은 해안으로 그 흐르는 모래사장 시원한 우물 옆
으로 가서 너를 내려놓을 수 있다면

Hysteria

I want to rip you apart with my teeth. I want to tear you to
death on this speeding subway. Hey, you groping, hey, hey,
hands off! I feel like I'm ripping, like I'll tear apart any second.
I want to scream, throw a fit, but I take my hand and push
deep into my gut. Breathe. Deep. Don't fucking touch me. I
said stop leaning on me. You're driving me nuts, what the fuck?
The leather of my body begins to strain. Is it a fox or a wolf?
I'm about to pop. Flowing blood like a lunar halo, bloodstains
that bleed through blue sheets, you think that's instinctual?
Because of the full moon? Shut your mouth. Truth-speaking
woman, if you know the truth, keep it to yourself. This is the
gospel of filthy humans. Periodic bleeding. Stomach cramps. I
won't stop. I'm complicated as hell, but people try and try to get
inside. I'm an insider, me. Not an outsider. You mumble even
in your sleep. Sudden hemorrhaging. Blood flowing. A world
with a big door. Closing, opening, repeat, repeat. A wheel that
stops and stops as it turns. I need a new route, need to get out.
I need a heavy duty maxi pad. What to do with this passed-
out-fucker? With his hand in my coat, this fucker is talking in
his sleep like he's reading a scribbled letter. I want to kill the
motherfucker. But what if he's my lover? If only I could pick
him up by the back of his neck with my teeth. I would leap off
this train and sprint over the tracks. I would head to the darkest
part of the night, my wild hair flapping. If only I could go to
the sandy beach on the red coast, moonlit. There, beside the
cool waters, I would lay him down. If only.

시골 창녀

진주에 기생이 많았다고 해도
우리 집안에는 그런 여자 없었다 한다
지리산 자락 아래 진주 기생이 이 나라 가장 오랜
기생 역사를 갖고 있다지만
우리 집안에 열녀는 있어도 기생은 없었단다
백정이나 노비, 상인 출신도 없는 사대부 선비 집
안이었다며 아버지는 족보를 외우신다
낮에 우리는 촉석루 앞마당에서 진주교방굿거리
춤을 보고 있었다
색한삼 양손에 끼고 버선발로 검무를 추는 여자
와 눈이 맞았다

집안 조상 중에 기생 하나 없었다는 게 이상하다
창가에 달 오르면 부푼 가슴으로 가야금을 뜯던
관비 고모도 없고
술자리 시중이 싫어 자결한 할미도 없다는 거
인물 좋았던 계집종 어미도 없었고
색색 비단을 팔러 강을 건너던 삼촌도 없었다는 거
온갖 멸시와 천대에 칼을 뽑아 들었던 백정 할아
비도 없었다는 말은
너무나 서운하다
국란 때마다 나라 구한 조상은 있어도 기생으로
팔려 간 딸 하나 없었다는 말은 진짜 쓸쓸하다

내 마음의 기생은 어디서 왔는가
오늘 밤 강가에 머물며 영감(靈感)을 뫼실까 하는
이 심정은
영혼이라도 팔아 시 한 줄 얻고 싶은 이 퇴폐를 어
찌할까
밤마다 칼춤을 추는 나의 유흥은 어느 별에 박힌
유전자인가

100

Country Whore

There were a lot of Jinju kisaeng
but I've been told our family didn't have any.
The Jinju kisaeng who lived under the skirts of Mt. Jiri
have the longest history
but our family had only chaste women. No kisaeng.
When Father reads from the family register
he lists nobles and scholars. No peasants, slaves, or merchants.
One afternoon we watched the Jinjukyobang shaman dance
in the Chokseoknu Pavillion.
I met the eyes of a woman performing a sword dance.
She was wearing socks and
traditional and brightly colored cloth covered her hands.

How did we not have any kisaeng in our family?
That we didn't have a government slave aunt
who plucked a gayakeum with a fluffed heart
when the moon rose by the window
a grandmother who killed herself because she didn't like
attending to drinking parties
a beautiful slave girl mother
an uncle who crossed rivers to peddle colorful silk
or a peasant grandfather who used
his sword out of contempt and scorn
is so disappointing.
How did we have an ancestor who saved the country
every time we faced an insurrection
but not a single daughter who was sold off to be a kisaeng?
It's depressing.
So where did the kisaeng in my mind come from?
Tonight by the river, I want to sell inspiration.
What to do with this decadence?
My decadence would sell my soul for a single line of a poem.
Which star is that gene stuck to?
My adult entertainment, sword dancing every night

나는 사채 이자에 묶인 육체파 창녀하고 다를 바
없다

나는 기생이다 위독한 어머니를 위해 팔려 간 소
녀가 아니다 자발적으로 음란하고 방탕한 감정 창녀
다 자다 일어나 하는 기분으로 토하고 마시고 다시
하는 기분으로 헝클어진 머리칼을 흔들며 엉망진창
여럿이 분위기를 살리는 기분으로 뭔가를 쓴다

다시 나는 진주 남강가를 걷는다 유등 축제가 열
리는 밤이다 취객이 말을 거는 야시장 강변이다 다
국적의 등불이 강물 위를 떠가고 떠내려가다 엉망진
창 걸려 있고 쏟아져 나온 사람들의 더러운 입김으
로 시골 장터는 불야성이다

부스스 펜을 꺼낸다 졸린다 펜을 물고 입술을 넘
쳐 잉크가 번지는 줄 모르고 코를 훌쩍이며 강가에
앉아 뭔가를 쓴다 나는 내가 쓴 시 몇 줄에 묶였다
드디어 시에 결박되었다고 믿는 미치광이가 되었다

눈앞에서 마귀가 바지를 내리고
빨면 시 한 줄 주지
악마라도 빨고 또 빨고, 계속해서 빨 심정이 된다

자다가 일어나 밖으로 나와 절박하지 않게 치욕적
인 감정도 없이
커다란 펜을 문 채 나는 빤다 시가 쏟아질 때까지
나는 감정 갈보, 시인이라고 소개할 때면 창녀라
고 자백하는 기분이다 조상 중에 자신을 파는 사람
은 없었다 '너처럼 나쁜 피가 없었다' 고 아버지는 말
씀하셨다
펜을 불끈 쥔 채 부르르 떨었다
나는 지금 지방 축제가 한창인 달밤에 늙은 천기
(賤技)가 되어 양손에 칼을 들고 춤춘다

I'm no different than a physical whore strapped
to the indenturement of a private loan.

I'm a kisaeng. But I'm not a girl sold off for her sick mother. I'm
a voluntarily obscene and debauched emotional whore. I wake
up with the feeling of having done it, so I puke and drink and do
it again. I shake my ruffled hair like a person coming to save the
mood of a party. In a mess, I write something.

I walk the south side of the Jinju river. Tonight is the Yu-deung
festival. Drunk people at the night market talk at me. National
flags painted on paper lamps float above. They fall into the river
and get tangled up. Lights float on the filthy breaths of people
who spill out of the country market. They give life to the night.

Disheveled and sleepy, I pull out my pen and bite. Unaware ink is
dripping from my lips, I sit by the riverside and write something.
I sob. I'm obsessed with the lines I write. I'm a madwoman who
finally believes she is bound to poetry.

The devil appears. He pulls down his pants in front of my eyes.
I'll give you a line if you give me a suck. Is he really the devil? Even
if he is, I will suck and suck and suck and suck and suck.

I sleep and wake and walk outside.
Without desperation, without shame
I bite a big pen and suck until poetry comes.
I'm an emotion slut.
When I say I'm a poet
it feels like I'm confessing I'm a whore.
No one in our family sold themselves, Father said
We never had blood like you.
I stroke my pen and shake violently.
I feel like an old filthy whore on a full-moon night
when the country festival is booming.
I'm dancing, a sword in each hand.

빈티지 소울

카메라 대신에 벽돌입니다 상자를 여니 벽돌 반
장이 나왔어요 믿을 수 없지만 깨끗한 벽돌입니다
왜 폴라로이드 카메라가 아니라 벽돌인지 물어보려
고 해도 연락두절이네요 인터넷 중고 시장을 통해
연결된 그 사람은 필름 10팩까지 끼워 거의 새것과
다름없는 카메라를 반값에 팔겠다고 했죠

힘주어 벽돌을 쥐고 흔들어봅니다 벽돌을 챙겨 들
고 집을 나섭니다 경찰서로 갈지 택배 송장에 적힌
주소지로 가야 할지 아직 모르겠어요

희미하게 어둠이 퍼져갑니다 보통 저녁입니다 골
백번의 골백번 더 살아본 날입니다 어이없고 참을
수 없이 분노가 치밀지만 똑같은 사기 사건도 수십
만번쨉니다 사소한 사기가 삶이었지요 예전엔 나귀
가죽하고 밀가루를 교환하다 시비가 붙어 칼에 찔
려 죽을 뻔했습니다 금화 몇 닢 받은 후 양피지를 보
내지 않은 적도 있고요

저 교회 벽돌도 내가 붙였습니다 나는 오래전 애
급에서 벽돌을 구워내던 노예, 무너지던 벽돌 더미
에 깔려 죽었겠지요 나는 사기 치다가 걸려 톱니바
퀴에서 고문당하던 상인, 콩고 강 하류에 던져진 번
제물, 언덕 꼭대기 대성당에서 목탄으로 모작을 그
리던 인부, 들판에서 나뭇잎으로 성기만 가리고 누
워 행인을 기다리는 창녀였을지 모릅니다

내 영혼은 중고품입니다 수거함에서 꺼낸 붉은 스
웨터처럼 팔꿈치가 닳고 닳은 영혼입니다 누군가 미
처 봉하지 못하고 떠나보낸 기억입니다 불현듯 바다
에서 솟아올랐거나 화산에서 흘러내린 먼지입니다

Vintage Soul

This is like a brick. It's not a camera. I open the box. There it is: half a brick. I can't believe this shit. A clean brick. I try to ask the seller, why the brick and not the Polaroid camera, but he's gone off the grid. I responded to his ad at an online marketplace for secondhand goods. He said he'd sell the camera good as new, half-price, and he'd throw in ten packs of film.

I clench the brick and try shaking it. Should I head to the police office or to the address on the invoice? I leave home holding the brick.

Darkness spreads dimly. It's a normal evening for me. I've lived this day over and over, hundreds and hundreds of times. It's ridiculous. My rage rises, almost out of control, but I've been through it all. This is the ten thousandth time I've been conned. It's all the same. Petty scams are my life. One time I got in a fight when I was trading donkey leather for flour. I was stabbed by a knife and almost died. Another time I received a couple gold coins for papyrus but I never sent the scroll.

I was the mason who built that church. I was a slave who baked bricks in Egypt. I died when a brick pile collapsed on me. Nobody knows who I might've been. A hustler merchant tortured on the wheel, a sacrifice thrown down the Congo river, a laborer who drew caricatures with charcoal on the side of a cathedral on a hill. Was I a whore lying on the grass waiting for passersby? Did I wear nothing but leaves to cover my genitals?

My soul is second-hand. It's like a red sweater with elbows that get worn out again and again, a memory shipped in a poorly sealed package, dust that suddenly surges up from the sea, dust that rolls down a volcano.

때때로 나는 처음으로 근사한 말을 떠올리지만 그 문장은 이미 내가 사막에서 벽돌을 굽다 지루해서 돌 위에 새겼던 말입니다 어딘가 처음 가보아도 언젠가 꼭 와서 살았던 곳 같습니다 내게 처음은 없지만 매 순간 처음처럼 화들짝 놀랍니다

당신이 왜 떠났는지 압니다 비애와 슬픔의 차이도 알고 저 모퉁이에서 걸어오던 사람이 왜 나한테 눈을 흘기고 가는지도 압니다 똑같은 일을 수십만 번 겪었으니까요 벽돌이 내게 온 이 상황에 대해서도 분개할 만한 일종의 흥미를 잃었습니다

하지만 건망증에 미달하는 기억력 때문에 나는 자신이 없습니다 카메라를 받기도 전에 선입금했고 또다시 사람을 믿었습니다 다행히 내 기억은 내 영혼은 약을 쳐야 기어 나오는 벌레 같아서 마치 없는 것처럼 또다시 누군가를 사랑할 것입니다

Sometimes a marvelous phrase pops into my mind for what I think is the first time. Then I remember that I already carved that sentence into a stone when I grew bored baking bricks in the desert. When I visit a place for the first time, I feel like I've lived there before. Even though I have no first times, every moment is a surprise, so they are all like first times for me.

I know why you left. I know the difference between grief and sadness and I know why that person in the corner stares at me when I pass. I've been through the same thing tens of thousands of times. Whenever I try to explain how I got a brick, I get lost in rage.

My memory hangs in absent-mindedness, so I lose my self-confidence. I made the payment before receiving the camera. I trusted people again. Fortunately my soul and memory are like bugs that only crawl out after pesticide is sprayed. It's like they never existed in the first place. That's why I'll re-learn to love people. I'm forgetful.

반불멸(反-不滅)

작은 전시관이야 예전에 너하고 봤던 그 그림들이야 「카페에서, 르탕부랭의 아고스티나 세가토리」 그 작품 생각나니? 반 고흐 애인으로 알려진 여자 초상화 말이야 근데 그 초상화 밑그림으로 다른 여자의 상반신이 그려져 있네 「포도」에도 「노란 장미가 담긴 잔」에도 다른 못 그린 그림들이 숨겨져 있어 가난한 화가가 재활용한 캔버스의 밑그림이 훤하게 보이는 거야 이렇게 회화에 엑스레이를 쐐보면 덧칠하기 전에 그린 그림들이 보인단 말이지 그가 덮어버린 스케치 감췄다고 믿었던 수많은 물감칠 안간힘 쓴 흔적들이 고스란히 들통 나는 거야

전시관 앞 기념품 가게 모퉁이에서 엽서에 몇 자 적어 보낸다 내가 죽거든 내 작품에 엑스레이나 전자현미경을 들이대지 마 낙서도 만화도 아닌 거 훔쳐본 누드 종이를 불에 그을려보지 마 덧칠한 시와 산문들 눈물이 마르지 않은 종이 위에 쓴 명랑한 노래 그지없이 한심한 필체나 지웠다가 쓰고 다시 덮어버린 잿빛 모래 위 갈매기 같은 글자를 보지 않길 바라 이걸 읽으며 넌 키득키득 웃어넘기겠지 한심한 네 작품을 누가 힘들여 분석하겠냐며 답장을 쓸지도 모르지 내가 죽거든 다시는 못 살아나게 지켜줘 내 얘길 하지도 마 일기든 메모든 수첩이든 불태워줘 약속해

Anti-Immortality

A small exhibition space. We saw these paintings together.
Do you remember *Agostina Segatori Sitting in the Café du
Tambourin?* It's a portrait of the woman thought to be Van
Gogh's lover. But the original sketch had the upper body of a
different woman. There are unfinished drawings hidden under
Grapes and *Glass with Yellow Roses* too. There are always bare
sketches on the recycled canvases of poor artists. When you
shoot an x-ray at the art you can see what they painted over.
Sketches the artist covered up, dabs of paint they erased, the
evidence of many desperate acts, everything gets exposed.

I'm at the gift shop at the front of the gallery, scribbling a few
words to you. Don't shove my work under an x-ray after I die.
No electronic microscopes. Not even if it's a doodle or cartoon.
Don't put a flame up to the paper nude I tried to steal. The
poetry and prose that I painted over, my merry songs written
on top of papers still wet with tears, the pitiful handwriting I
erased, wrote again and covered up, words like seagulls on ash
and sand, don't look at any of it. Reading this you may laugh,
hahaha. Perhaps you want to write back, *Who would go through
the trouble of analyzing your pathetic work that deeply?* But please
protect me from resurrection. Don't talk about me after I die.
Journals, memos, notebooks, whatever. Burn them. Promise.

JUDITH
SANTOPIETRO

TIAWANAKU

POEMAS DE LA MADRE COQA
POEMS FROM THE MOTHER COQA

TRANSLATED BY ILANA LUNA

Tiawanaku: Poems from the Mother Coqa

by Judith Santopietro
Translated from the Spanish by Ilana Luna
Orca Libros; 2019

Tiawanaku: Poems from the Mother Coqa (Orca Libros, 2019), written by Judith Santopietro and translated by Ilana Luna, takes readers on a very personal journey through the Bolivian and Peruvian Andes. Through Judith's voice, we become observers and participants of the geographical and cultural landscapes, and the contemporary lives of indigenous communities. The center of this collection is Tiawanaku, a sacred ancestral site in Bolivia. With lucidity and humor, she explores the relationship between indigenous cultures and globalized media, the validity of millenary traditions in a hybrid, peripheral modernity, and the experience of multilingualism. The complexity with which these issues are juxtaposed in the collection helps break down stereotypes about indigenous identities, especially women's, and dismantles the idea that indigenous peoples are marginal.

Orca Libros is a publishing collective created in 2018 in the U.S. by women of diverse ethnic, national and professional backgrounds, including writers, translators, academics and artists. Our work has been shaped by sorority, and the desire to make literature by women from the Americas and literature that engages ethnic and linguistic minorities available to a wider audience. We are convinced of the value of collective creativity in the face of literary markets that have historically been determined by the whims of corporate publishing and the media circuits that feed the industry. We believe it is possible to challenge these structures, and, in our case, to overcome language and circulation barriers for Latin American women, or U.S. Latinas, whose work has a limited scope within the U.S. We think everyone has a right to read diverse literature in translation, not just the *New York Times* bestsellers.

Since 2018 we have published two books of poetry, bilingually: *Sordera de las nieves* (2018) by Lina X. Aguirre, translated by Richard Gordon, and *Tiawanaku: Poemas de la Madre Coqa*. In 2021, we plan to publish two novels, first in the original language, and later in translation. It is our mission not just to provide excellent original works, but to focus on the careful craft of translating. We adopt this dual approach, on the one hand, because our authors, as well as their works, are immersed in linguistically hybrid worlds; and, on the other, because we want our readers to have access not just to words-as-signs on paper, but also to the whole perceivable universe that surrounds them. We believe that the great capacity to affect us that is present in the literature produced by women can be maintained in the transit between languages if and when the translation is founded on the profound connection between translator and writer and the act of empathy through listening and accompaniment.

In the case of *Tiawanaku*, this journey of translation-listening-empathy, took place as author, translator and editor together holed ourselves up in a cabin in the

Sierra Madre of Oaxaca (México), where we exchanged stories and ideas, re-wrote, walked for hours beneath hail, and sipped mezcal in front of the hearth, warmed by the burning embers. We ate in community dining halls of the autonomous indigenous communities, took part in a ritual cleansing and a temazcal (sweat lodge), laughed ourselves silly and cried our shared pain in order to create the book, together, as a multilingual and culturally plural whole. The majority of the translation took place in this collective space, and once the translation was drafted, together we read the work out loud, in both languages, discussed different concepts and terms, and listened for rhythms and unintentional cacophonies. At times, the translation led to modifications of the source text, as in the case of the Aymara woman taking a selfie.

At the end of this process, we created a trilingual glossary of Aymara and Quechua terms to allow for a more extensive explanation of Andean cosmogonies without interrupting the flow of the poems, and to foreground the influence of living languages over colonial tongues. In *Tiawanaku*, Judith Santopietro invokes a physical space, sometimes brutal and cold, that exposes readers to the daily struggle for cultural survival in the face of global forces that extract resources and sell the image of the indigenous, only to leave the real people, porters of millenary cultures, in oblivion. Thus, our decision to translate the subtitle of the book as 'Poems from the Mother Coqa,' as if 'la madre coqa' were a place rather than a person. We also decided to write the name of the plant 'coqa' with a 'q' in order to distinguish its cultural use from the drug term 'coke' that has caused so much damage in our Americas. We also chose to retain metric descriptions of the geographies and mountain peaks, despite the fact that in the English-speaking world the metric system is not used with as much frequency, as it was important to us to maintain the feeling of penetrating a geographical space with its own particular sociocultural history. The sacred town of Tiawanaku is not a mere backdrop; it is the reason for this poetry's existence.

Lina Aguirre, Orca Libros

Kalasasaya

Aún las piedras verticales en esta pampa
el aire que habita los pasillos
caras pétreas en un templo de paredes ocres

Aún así   extiendo los brazos a distancias que no puedo mirar:
caigo por esta cumbre
sostengo la navaja en una mano
         con la otra   percibo el corazón y sus rugidos
         detengo las injurias que erosionan mi boca

esta es la tierra donde no nací
su desfile polvoriento me fastidia
sus imperios del racismo me son indiferentes

Aún   la cruz Chakana marca el Sur y sus misterios:
Jach'a Qhana   que es rosa de los vientos y cráter
nido de cóndores que sobrevuelan la estepa lunar

Aún así   me deleitan las sangrantes cabecitas
poso junto a cada rictus
que asoma en las paredes del templete
fotografías con rostros modelados en tercera dimensión

              (la aymara Hilaria Sejas, flamante alcaldesa,
                  filma un anuncio para la televisión,
           el reflector platina su sombrero de bombín y la pollera)

A distancias que no puedo mirar
las piedras erguidas en medio del templo
una estela luce vestida de andesita:
aún el fraile monolito acicala sus cangrejos
gordo y con los dedos torcidos por la artritis
prepara el mate   *estito está estiando*   dice cuando el agua borbotea
y vierte ardor sobre la coqa

Kalasasaya

And yet the vertical stones in this grassland
the air inhabiting the passageways
stone faces in an ochre-walled temple

Even still   I stretch my arms beyond where I can see:
I fall from this peak
I hold the blade in one hand
                        with the other   I feel the heart and its roar
                        I hold back the injuries that erode my mouth

this is the land where I wasn't born
its dusty parade wearies me
I'm indifferent to its empires of racism

And yet   the Chakana cross marks the South and its mystery:
Jach'a Qhana   the windrose and crater
the nest of condors that fly above this lunar steppe

Even still   I'm delighted by its tiny bloodied heads
I pose beside each grimace
that peaks out from the walls of the shrine
photographs with faces sculpted in three dimensions

                        (the Aymara woman Hilaria Sejas, flamboyant mayor,
                                films a commercial for the television,
                                the reflector shines her bowler hat and *pollera*)

Farther than my eye can see
the upright stones in the center of the temple
a stela dressed like andesite
still the monolithic friar scrubs his crabs
fat and with twisted arthritic fingers
he prepares the tea   *the thingy is thinging*   he says when the water bubbles
and he pours burning heat on coqa leaves

a veces llora en arenisca peces
y su fluido colma cada gárgola
limpia las columnas   abre la puerta al inicio temporal del Sol:
así de primavera el equinoccio

Pero los dioses que observan las estrellas
escuchan mi voz en los rincones de la estancia
con un tímpano secreto entre las rocas:

esta es una tierra donde no nací
su desfile polvoriento me fastidia
sus imperios del racismo me son indiferentes

extiendo   los brazos   a distancias   que no puedo   narrar:

caigo   por esta áspera cumbre

navaja en mano

escucho los rugidos que desgajan el hielo de los Andes.

sometimes he cries on sandstone fish
and his excretion floods each gargoyle
he cleans the columns   opens the door to the temporal initiation of the Sun:
just like the spring equinox

But the gods who observe the stars
they hear my voice in the corners of the room
with a secret eardrum among the rocks:

>   *this is a land where I wasn't born*
>   *its dusty parade wearies me*
>   *I'm indifferent to its empires of racism*

I stretch   my arms   beyond   my ability   to narrate:

I fall   on this ragged peak

blade in hand

I hear the roars that shear off the ice of the Andes.

Puma Punku

(primeros rituales)

La estría de mi lengua
serpiente que se arrastra sobre la pampa
        hiere la franja de una luz aguda

Desnuda en la orilla
con la carne que palpita en tundra
observo desde un monte
por el espectro de mi ojo

Puma Punku   o la puerta fundida en jugos vegetales
del bronce al granito cuárzico
        de la andesita virgen al basalto
                de la cantera líquida al azufre sideral

Es el ascenso de este amor que ocurre al mediodía
cuando el azogue se transforma en sangre
y mi sangre en vasija donde crece un nido
poblado de reptiles y semillas

así que imploro:

   mesa de las ofrendas
                        lana pigmentada de las llamas
diminutas flores en el rito
               chispas del alcohol absoluto que se incendia

en el ritual convocas:

   Ekeko   señor voluptuoso
                    que tu falo preñe los billetes falsos
señor del rayo a cuestas
            señor de la joroba   de la abundancia erótica

Puma Punku

(initiating rituals)

The striations of my tongue
a serpent that slides across the grasslands
           wounding the edge of a sharp light

naked on the banks
with flesh that pulses on tundra
I watch from the mountain
with the specter of my eye

Puma Punku   or the door melted in vegetable acids
from bronze to quartz granite
      from the virgin andesite to basalt
         from the liquid quarry to the sidereal sulfur

It's the ascent of this love that transpires at midday
when the quicksilver becomes blood
and my blood in the vessel where a nest grows
inhabited by reptiles and seeds

so I implore:

   table of offerings
                  pigmented llama wool
miniscule ritual flowers
         flickers of absolute alcohol set alight

during the rite you summon:

   Ekeko   voluptuous lord
             may your phallus impregnate the false bills
   lord of the uphill lightning
        hunchback lord   of erotic abundance

En los primeros rituales
pronuncio este vocablo que seduce
la lluvia de septiembre
su savia escurre en copos
como orina inesperada de los dioses
acontece la tormenta de las cuatro eras
más tarde el diluvio andino se evapora.

In the initiating rituals
I pronounce this word that seduces
September's rain
its sap drips in flakes
like an unexpected pissing of the gods
the tempest of the four eras occurs
later the Andean deluge evaporates.

Piedra   de piedra nacen

rígidos y lujuriosos por la noche
con el gesto irónico y el mismo nervio
que parte desde el cráneo

Arena   de la arenisca vienen
por las venas pulsátiles
los dioses en éxodo bajan el sendero
                    azul de la montaña
deambulan en angiomas eréctiles
por la vereda filiforme

Stone   From Stone They Are Born

rigid and lecherous at night
with the ironic gestures and the same nerve
that runs down from the skull

Sand   from the sandstone they come
for the pulsating veins
the gods in exodus go down the blue
                        path of the mountain
they wander in erectile angiomas
along the threadlike trail

Desciendo Tiawanaku

en el tiempo de su ch'alla
            ofrenda que navega por los ríos del altiplano

Desciendo Tiawanaku
y en la ciudad un anciano atrae la lluvia exuberante con su tarqha
            el sonido cavernoso de esa flauta gotea
hasta este paraje estercolado de la humanidad.

I Descend Tiawanaku

in the time of the ch'alla
            an offering that navigates the rivers of the altiplano

I descend Tiawanaku
and in the city an old man summons the exuberant rain with his tarqha
                        the cavernous sound of that flute drips
all the way to this manure-filled expanse of humanity.

Pijcheo

La bruma sobre tus labios Khana Willka
me ofreces una bolsa hinchada con pétalos de coqa
y la lejía amplifica el sabor para el pijcheo

también ceniza sobre tus ojos
con los dientes verduscos cortas los peciolos
me das los alcaloides limpios
evito quejarme en los pasillos de la terminal
aunque el mal de altura persiste desde la frontera

una vez en la habitación del Perla Negra   frente a la estación
regurgito pesadillas de cuchillas lanzadas desde los matorrales
una persecución militar en las conexiones alteradas de mi mente

hay armas que jamás se disparan
algunos niños escondidos en los cañaverales

hay tallos retorcidos que sepultan sus cuerpos
la coqa aminora los efectos del soroche
            náusea   casi muerte súbita al caminar
            angustia de cabalgata en el pecho

la adrenalina fluye en ese sueño
también mi curiosidad botánica por reconocer
cada filamento de las plantas y el arte de domesticarlas
inquisitiva por saber
        a quién pertenecen las uñas desprendidas en el fango
        a quién la dermis carcomida por hormigas rojas
con qué refinada técnica los desaparecieron

el jugo sobre tus labios   Khana Willka
me devuelve a la geografía del hotel
mascamos el bolo vegetal hasta que nos contiene
nos sumerge en el espacio de los sin nombre.

Pijcheo

The haze over your lips Khana Willka
you offer me a bag stuffed with coqa petals
and the lye amplifies their flavor for the pijcheo

and ashes over your eyes too
with greenish teeth you cut the leafstalks
you give me cleaned alkaloids
I try not to whimper in the corridors of the terminal
even though the elevation sickness has persisted since the border

once we're in the Black Pearl bedroom   facing the station
I regurgitate dreams of blades thrown from the brush
a military persecution in the altered connections of my mind

there are weapons that never fire
some children that hide in the cane fields

there are twisted stalks that bury their corpses
the coqa relieves the effects of the soroche
            nausea   practically sudden death from walking
                anguish from the galloping in your chest

adrenaline flows through this dream
also my botanical curiosity to recognize
each filament of the plants and the art of domesticating them
inquisitive to know
        to whom these detached nails in the swamp belong
        to whom the epidermis consumed by red ants
with what refined technique they were disappeared

the juice on your lips   Khana Willka
returns me to the geography of the hotel
we chew the vegetable cud until it contains us
it plunges us into the same place as the no-names.

Reino mineral de náuseas

Parece un glaciar derritiéndose sobre la lumbre   pero es fiebre   Un
reino mineral de náuseas que me hace vomitar sin tregua   me envuelve
en espasmos y luminiscencias en el iris   un sonido puntiagudo borra la
visión   Hospitalizada varios días   semanas o años   fraguo los planes
del suicidio: un salto leve desde un techo donde mirar las ramas más
altas de los árboles   las espadas de fuego rompen y diluyen las venas
Desde la habitación   redacto correos electrónicos y notas transparentes
en mis cuadernos: llegan memorias filosas   madrugadas en que
desciendo la serranía en medio de un huracán   los ríos desbordados
cruzan la ciudad   quizá un secuestro   Desde la habitación   heredo y
reacomodo bienes que no tengo   rompo cartas y escritos imaginarios
Decido regresar a mi apartamento y desaparecer porque mi voz no cabe
en el dolor de este país.

Mineral Kingdom of Nausea

It seems like a glacier melting over the fire   but it's a fever   A mineral
kingdom of nausea that makes me vomit without rest   it wraps me in
spasms and luminosities of the iris   a sharp sound that blurs my vision
Hospitalized for several days   weeks or years   I forge a suicide plan: a
simple jump from a rooftop from which to see the tallest branches of
the trees   the fiery swords break and dilute my veins   From inside
the room   I draft emails and transparent notes in my diaries: sharp
memories appear   breaking dawns in which I descend the mountain
in the middle of a hurricane   the overflowing rivers cut across the city
maybe a kidnapping   From inside the room   I will and redistribute
possessions that I don't own   I rip up imaginary letters and writings
I decide to return to my apartment and disappear because my voice
doesn't fit into this country's pain.

YANG LIAN 楊煉

ANNIVERSARY SNOW

translated by **Brian Holton** & others

Anniversary Snow

by Yang Lian
Translated from the Chinese by Brian Holton with further translations by W.N.
Herbert, L. Leigh, Liang Lizhen, Pascale Petit, Fiona Sampson, George Szirtes and
Joshua Weiner
Shearsman Books; 2019

Yang Lian is a poet from China, who lives in exile – currently in Germany, but
previously in New Zealand, Australia, and the U.K. Recognised today as one
of the most powerful voices in contemporary Chinese poetry, he first came to
prominence as a member of the group known as the 'Misty Poets', who gathered
around the literary journal *Jintian* (*Today*), founded in Beijing in 1978 by Mang
Ke and Bei Dao. The group's poetry was referred to as 'misty' because their work
was felt to be obscure, particularly by contrast with the socialist-realist poetry that
was espoused by official cultural outlets at the time. His work was formally banned
in 1989 after he organised memorial services for the dead of Tiananmen Square
while on a visit to New Zealand. Yang Lian has lived outside China since 1989, but
is able to return to his homeland, and his works have been published in several
volumes in Shanghai.

At Shearsman, we have published two anthologies edited by Yang Lian, as well
as two volumes of his own poetry (including *Anniversary Snow*) — both of which
are gatherings of uncollected poems, rather than the long sequences for which he
has become well known and which have been published by Bloodaxe in the U.K.
Anniversary Snow does however contain some shorter sequences alongside single
poems. Yang Lian is fortunate to have a regular translator of great skill in Brian
Holton, and this is one of reasons why — along with Bei Dao, who also lives in
exile — he is the most published contemporary Chinese poet in English.

At Shearsman we have a distinct preference for the developmental 'line' that
begins with Anglo-American modernism, and with Franco-Spanish surrealism,
and feel that Yang's work fits very neatly on that line, notwithstanding the
inevitable cultural differences arising from very different literary traditions.
Yang's work has inevitably felt some influence from Western models, and he has
spoken admiringly of Ezra Pound's work, for instance, but he is also constantly
in dialogue with the far-reaching Chinese literary tradition. As with the other
'Misty' poets, Yang has tended to use free verse — albeit with a marked attention
to rhythm and other structural elements — rather than classical forms, but his
work in this volume often does employ rhyme, sometimes spectacularly, as Brian
Holton notes somewhat ruefully in his Afterword to the book: ruefully, because
the more spectacular performances inevitably resist equivalences in English. I
would recommend that interested readers find sound recordings or videos of the
poet online so as to get a sense of the way he manipulates sound patterns in the
original texts — they can be extraordinary.

On this occasion, not *all* the translations are by Brian Holton. The book also gathers up some versions made by British and American poets who have worked with Yang Lian to create versions in English, albeit usually without having any Chinese themselves. Yang likes to work this way in addition to the regular method of professional scholarly translation, believing that a true poet can see the intent of the original, even without a native command of the language in which it is written.

Anniversary Snow comes in an unusual square format — mainly to cope with the long lines employed in the translations, as we wanted to avoid the many carry-overs that the lines would have required in a more conventional format. Recommendations for further reading of Yang Lian's work: *Concentric Circles* and *Narrative Poem*, both from Bloodaxe, *Riding Pisces* (containing earlier work) from Shearsman and *Yi* (a long poem that engages with the ancient *I Ching*) from Green Integer.

Tony Frazer, Shearsman Books

舞：和李白裸泳

一

清晨五点　　这城市是乌鸦的
天踮着发亮的脚尖　　叫喊一片黑
水做的羽毛给你披挂空的
华彩　　泉眼中曙光淋漓
昨夜都是漩涡

二

名字里一小块碎月
凌乱的白　　谁不是那白
醉的孤寂把我看成两个　　十个
百万个　　裸出影子的你
纵身入水的姿势何等繁华

三

夜光杯掷成玻璃塔楼的高脚杯
花丛每瓣是橱窗　　而眉眼之
媚　　再脱也脱不掉
酒香倒映中　　舞步摇摇欲坠
公主的厌倦非时空的热烈

四

复数的指尖探入复数的皮肤
揉动　　就划动一朵白云
复数的肥嫩的河　　浮泛月之绿
一朵螺钿的银花就亲近到腮边
濡湿的天空又留在身下

五

舞蹈剥光舞者
乌鸦在某处叫　　你的黑暗斟满
你自己　　一行诗泼溅出一种

134

Dance: Swimming Naked With Li Bai

'My dancing shadow is all over the place'

1

five in the morning   this town belongs to the crows
the sky stands on shining tiptoe   yelling blackness
feathers of water put on for you empty
beauty   dawn dripped wetly from the spring's mouth
last night was all whirlpool

2

little fragment of broken moon in a name
bedraggled white   who isn't that white
booze's loneliness takes me for two   ten
millions of   you that bares your shadow
how ravishing the gesture of leaping into water

3

a thrown Nightgleam Cup turns into the tall goblet of a glass tower
each petal in the bouquet a display case   brow and eye's
charm   no matter how you try can't be shed
booze's bouquet in reflections   dance steps totter unsteadily
a princess's weariness is the passion of non-spacetime

4

plural fingertips explore in plural skin
kneading   to paddle a white cloud
plural fat and tender river   green with floating moons
a silver flower of abalone gets up close to a cheek
soaking sky again left under you

5

the dance strips the dancer bare
crows somewhere caw   your darkness fills
your self   a line of verse spatters some kind of

公主的醉态　　从唐朝斜倚过来
孤寂　　没有踩偏的脚步

六
一盏酒浇铸喉咙的造型
一个最私密的　　暴露于众目的动作
摇荡器官　　缺陷炫目而美
一次跳进河的腥香　　水淋淋
一千年潜泳于那腥香

七
这首诗里影子在说话　　影子
披着无常　　看月和光相反流淌
水面上一支音乐和世界相反流淌
影子幻想中
捣毁等于存在

八
于是公主没有实体的脖子
有不减退的　　被勒断的疼
于是一个早晨的天青色　　随乌鸦
起舞　　霓裳羽衣弃置岸边
诗人想穿就穿上那体温

九
举杯　　邀雪白沉醉的晶体
邀　　翩翩来也翩翩去的爱
邀你成为我　　而我久已是她
孤独是复数的浸泡彼此的性
翩翩　　同一杯酒骑上一万朵牡丹

十
天空中大团舞蹈的肉色
旋入这畅饮　　掩映中不散的春意
旋入诗意　　影子不疲倦的激情
一壶倾倒不尽的色情
你　　（或我）　　逃不出磨人之纯

136

princess's drunkenness   sprawling aslant from Tang times
loneliness   has no mistaken feet to trample everywhere

6

one glass of booze is cast in the throat's mould
a most private act   exposed to public view
rocks internal organs   blemish is beauty and glory
jump once into the river's fishy stink   then soaking wet
dive a thousand years beneath that fishy stench

7

In this poem shadow is speaking   shadow
wears impermanence   sees moon and light in contraflow
on the water a piece of music and world in contraflow
shadow imagining
destruction equal to existence

8

so the princess's neck has no reality
has a pain that never ebbs   the pain of strangling it broken
so the sky blue of one morning   along with the crows
dancing   rainbow skirt and feather cloak discarded on the banking
a poet will wear that body temperature if he wants to

9

raise a glass   invite drunken and snow-white crystal
invite   love that lightly comes and lightly goes
invite you to be me   but I've been her for a long time
loneliness is plural soaking in each other's sex
lightly   the same glass mounts ten thousand peonies

10

in the sky a great ball of dancing flesh tones
whirl into this drinking spree   contrast with unsundering first love
whirling into poetry   shadow's unwearying desire
a jug of endlessly pouring passion
you   (or I)   can't escape from a painful purity

十一
甜蜜如非人的　　我们看不见
时间　　只把时间带在体内
公主渐渐变蓝的欲望带着此刻
醒或醉　　轮换一点点失重
足够忘却上一个开端

十二
乌鸦顺着裸体流下
城市顺着裸体流下
水的叫声　　黑透你也在亮透你
让我一根根数清金黄的阴毛
又一个宇宙刚刚清洁了舞台

杨炼
2010, 10, 18——2011, 2, 21

11
sweet as something inhuman   we can't see
time   only carry it in itself
the princess's desire slowly blues with carrying moments
drunk or sober   taking more and more turns at weightlessness
enough to forget the last beginning

12
crows cascade down nakedness
the town cascades down nakedness
the cry of water   blackens you and brightens you
makes me count golden pubic hairs one by one
another universe has just cleared the dance floor

18 October 2010–21 February 2011

嵌死的小史诗

晚点的镜子　　取消的天空
嵌死的窗户外　　跑道像座水族馆
夜航灯衬着夜雨的反光双倍漂泊
一种无声　　保持着压力
　　　　　吮啊　　你像个降落的小海
　　　　　骑上一枚舌尖　　分泌甜甜的黑暗
错位的时间也不顾一切地漫漶
四溢　　嘴对嘴嵌着呼喊的缝
把飞不尽的天边　　叠进床单的皱褶
把一支送别歌　　绕过女孩那么玲珑的肩头
同一朵送别的云含着
　　　　　双腿的肉翼　　扑搧在身体两旁
　　　　　眺望嵌死的夜色
　　　　　扑入无须出路的激情的奇花
我们用躯体　　张挂全世界血红的航班
最美妙的推迟　　推迟成现在
镜子倒映　　咫尺之外摸不到的水渍
都银亮亮汪在身下
　　　　　吮你　　嫩蕊似的源头
　　　　　紧紧拢住　　无限绽开　　那四面八方
只有这一岸　　嵌死在一只鸟的想象里
想象这房间追着一场海啸
温柔的开关藏在海底
飞机场　　一只爱的节拍器
指挥飞的一生　　向一次涌起冲刺
　　　　　一次颤颤萌芽的坠毁　　黏在
　　　　　舌尖尽头　　指尖尽头
　　　　　你的幽暗中　　每个点都像诗　　一碰就生长
呼救的巢　　扔在哪儿都孵出宇宙
我们彼此像光年　　彼此在射程之内
再香死一次仍挣不脱裸露的轮回
　　　　　夜航灯滑过　　房间忽明忽暗如鬼魅
　　　　　嵌死进浩渺　　带我们

Deeply Embedded Little Epic

a delayed mirror   cancelled sky
beyond a deeply embedded window   aquarium-like runway
navigation lights set against reflections of night rain doubly drifting
a kind of soundlessness   keeping pressure up
       oh sucking   you're like a little touched-down ocean
       riding on a tongue tip   secreting a sweet darkness
and dislocated time blurs regardless
overflows   mouth to mouth embedded in the roaring seam
folding a sky line you can't fly to the end of   into creases on a bed sheet
bypasses farewell songs   round a girl-like so exquisite shoulder
one identical farewell cloud contains
       flesh wings of legs   slapping each side of the body
       seeing deeply embedded night from afar away
       slapping strange flowers of passion that need no way out
we use our bodies   to hang up all the world's blood red flights
the most wonderful postponement   postponed into now
the mirror reflects   unreachable damp patches inches away
poured silvery bright alongside us
       sucking you   a tender bud-like fountainhead
       held firm   endlessly unfolds   in all directions
with only this shore   deeply embedded in a bird's imagination
imagining this room chasing a tidal wave
a gentle switch hidden in the seabed
airport   a metronome of love
conducting a lifetime of flying   sprint toward a single spurting
       one single crash of trembling germination   stuck to
       the very tips of tongues   the very tips of fingers
       in your dark   each dot like a poem   grows as it touches
a nest crying for help   thrown anywhere could hatch a universe
we're like light years from each other   each within firing range
deeply aromatic once again yet can't win free of naked reincarnation
       navigation lights slip by   the spectral room now dark now bright
       deeply embedded in vastness   it leads us

全力以赴投奔那浩渺
从头到尾是一首诗　　寻觅着形体
荡漾着形体　　它在这　　微亮磷光的边缘
完美如时间一再漏掉的东西

to go all out to seek shelter in that vastness
from top to tail it's a poem   seeking form
rippling through a form   it is here   with faintly phosphorescent edge
a thing perfect as time leaked out again and again

维罗纳的雨声

每一滴小小的透明的心形
都会碎　　与朱丽叶无关的碎
每块粉红色大理石　　插着箭
诺言湿漉漉降了半旗

游客懒洋洋的　　午餐也是
叉尖上一小片肉对称于
脚下的流水　　伞像枝眉笔
扫着云　　在维罗纳谁不会忧郁？

谁没被初恋洗得醉醺醺？
雨声的叠字让成对的身体
更粘　　叠韵再发明一个吻
广场上淅淅沥沥的叠句

把你放在我对面　　那儿
就是阳台　　天空的铁梯子
有命运的慌乱　　鱼骨听你说
来呀　　发白呀　　我们这只梨

总是刚从影子里剥出的
也只把最有味儿的爱给影子
诗在我对面　　比但丁高一点
某裙裾正晕眩地抽出雨丝

比石雕的鹰眼高出一点
某纤巧　　某粉红　　微露着脚趾
声音的玻璃鞋毁灭般轻盈
从一滴飞踩上另外一滴

雨声是雨的影子　　只一瞥
这场雨就得永远下　　这首诗
就得像一笔债用毕生偿还
当我里面的空　　渴望着加倍

The Voice of Rain in Verona

each drop of tiny transparent heart shapes
will shatter   fragments that have nothing to do with Juliet
every bit of pink marble   arrow-pierced
a promise that falls dripping to half-mast

tourists are lethargic   so is lunch
a little bit of meat on the tines of a fork symmetrical with
running water underfoot   umbrellas like eyebrow pencils
sweep the clouds   who wouldn't be melancholy in Verona?

who hasn't been washed clean of drunkenness by first love?
reduplicated syllables of rain make paired bodies
stickier still   as rhyme invents a kiss again
a pitter-patter refrain in the square

puts you in front of me   there
it's the balcony   the iron ladder of the sky
preordained panic   fish bones hear you say
oh come   oh turn pale   we are a pear

always new-peeled from shadow
and always giving the tastiest love to shadows
the poem in front of me   loftier than Dante
some skirt dizzily pulling out the drizzling rain

higher than the carved stone eagle's eye
a certain delicacy   a certain pink   toes hardly shown
glass slipper of voices elegant as destruction
tread in flight on one drop and another

the voice of rain is rain's shadow   just one glimpse
this shower must be forever falling   this poem
must seem a debt repaid for a lifetime
as the void in me   longs to be double

你就被丢在爱情中间
一只铜乳房任男孩们放肆地
扣弄　　一个快门烧焦的
天堂的现在不进行时

用尽了鲜艳　　却还鲜艳着
雨中的但丁中学生似的痴迷
被罂粟花小小的器官逼着
爱　　　上　　温柔的缺陷的知识

缺陷引领一首诗　　向上
那不会完美的　　驱策你完美
雨声　　教我聆听不在的
维罗纳　　人都是开采殆尽的?

唱过　　吻过　　死过　　写过
在一座舞台上叠入彼此
背诵的时代　　当台词包扎起
伤口　　无视缺陷　　哪来诗?

爱剥出一个难忍的陌生的
我　　光束下石头会呼吸
你的眼神滑过　　云纹
在我肉里发苦　　我已是

几乎制成的　　接到那口信
某流去流入某场音乐会
碎着血色素细细摆放的碎
没有退路　　迎着你升起

then you are left in the midst of love
a bronze breast lets boys wantonly
stroke   a heavenly present tense
charred by the camera shutters

bright beauty used up   but brightly hued still
Dante in the rain fascinated like a high school student
forced by the poppy's tiny viscera
to fall   in love   with knowledge of gentle flaws

flaws guide a poem   upwards
it won't be perfect   impelling you to perfection
rain's voice   teaches me to listen closely to what isn't there
in Verona   has everyone else been totally exploited?

sung   kissed   killed   written
folded into each other on stage
an age of recitation   as actors' lines bandage
wounds   ignore flaws   where is poetry from?

love peels an unendurable unfamiliar
me   stones will breathe in rays of light
your gaze has slid over   moiré clouds
turns bitter in my flesh   I'm now

almost manufactured   got the message
a certain outward flow in a certain concert of music
shattering plainly-arranged fragments of haemoglobin
no way back   facing your rise

超前研究

（赠 Adonis）

一，舔之时刻

爬山虎的红叶　　失血
舔着雪意

舔它　　你的舌头存在吗？
　　　　我们的舌头存在吗？

死去的母亲怀抱这扇小窗
死后还在躲藏
嗜好叛卖的　　涂抹进大屠杀的地点

藤蔓指爪下　　铁蒺藜抓碎的肉存在吗？

沿着湖岸走　　死亡有甜丝丝的味儿
沿着深秋走　　铁栅栏箍紧灯下的词
散开的词　　砸在母亲脸上的枪托
灰烬的风景中一道眼神仍贴着铁轨
滑行　　一九三三　　一九八九　　二零零一

得多冷漠　　才能忍住一枚红叶
摇曳　　杀戮的美？

148

Advanced Study

for Adonis

1. A Moment of Licking

ivy's red leaves   haemorrhage
licking the smell of imminent snow

lick it   does your tongue exist?
        do our tongues exist?

dead mothers embrace this little window
still in hiding after death
a place addicted to betrayal   smeared with massacres

beneath the vine's claws   does barbed-wire-torn flesh exist?

walking by the lake   death has a sweet and happy taste
walking by deep autumn   iron railings tightly girdle lamplit words
scattered words   smash rifle butts in mothers' faces
in a landscape of ash the gaze still fixes on a railway line
coasting   1933   1989   2001

how uncaring must you be to bear a single red leaf
brandishing   the beauty of butchery?

二，穿行：铜与玻璃之书

铜的词典衍生出书法　　你选择
大英博物馆张开虚空　　无视我们相依走过
一只玉辟邪回头　　无视海浪的钴蓝
精雕细刻　　璀璨如大马士革

晦暗如大马士革　　一张六千年的底片
含着树木　　女诗人的葱绿间　　那美少年
含着化学　　躺进成排灰色的孩子
一只只玻璃柜子无声震碎　　被某一天

每一天　　提炼出不呼吸的性质
玉辟邪耸起双耳　　聆听地平线那缕血丝
沁缝达豪　　查理检查站　　耶路撒冷
烛火湿而粘　　每个母亲都会流泪

母亲们静静清点反光里的人影
忘　　无形爆炸　　恒温计调控的立方中
母亲不会再变白的头发　　恐怖地变黑
衬着拉马拉街角上一盏瞎透的灯

日夜照射相依而行的鬼魅
辉煌如双行诗　　你刚拈回的玫瑰
一股地狱味儿　　冲洗一页页冷凝的疼
我们向下　　迎娶继续大出血的新月

2. Walk Through: Books of Bronze and Glass

calligraphy born from a lexicon of bronze   your choice
the British Museum opens a void   ignores us   as we walk by arm in arm
a piece of jade wards off repentance   ignores the cobalt blue of the ocean waves
carved with a sculptor's precision   dazzling as Damascus

dark as Damascus   a six-thousand-year photographic plate
contains trees   amongst the loden green of a poetess   that Adonis
contains chemistry   lies down into a row of grey children
glass cases silently shaken to pieces   by a certain day

every day   extracts unbreathingness
jade wards off both high-rise ears   intent on hearing the blood-streaked skyline
leaching out of cracks in Dachau   Checkpoint Charlie   Jerusalem
candle flame wet and sticky   every mother will shed tears

in silence mothers tick off reflected shadows
forget   imperceptible explosions   in the thermostat control cube
mothers' hair that will never turn white again   goes terrifyingly black
sets off a stone-blind lamp post on a Ramallah street corner

shining day and night on monsters walking arm-in-arm
glorious as a ghazal   the rose you just pinched back
a whiff of the stench of hell   washing page after page of congealed pain
downward we   marry the haemorrhaging moon

三，诗学探讨——另一个嵌入的声音

不能真   是不是美的错？
        想象一件河底撒开的衬衣
    浸进柏林秋夜的黑
        想象那双眼睛呛满水   水呛满母亲
谁说死不是湿淋淋的和声？
    河底的小窗亮着那演奏
    河底   一个不停跃下的词
            不停找到漏下的呜咽
    叶子向下而伤口向上
        房子向下   品尝的雪意向上
舌尖   钩住的毁灭是否远远不够？
            想象一个滚落的自我
        呛满历史的黑水   滚落如卵石
        没别的时间除了抽缩的肺
        没别的语法除了剥开生命那件衬衣
说   死侧身人形的茫茫
再淤积是否仍然不够？
            沉溺之诗里只有正在到来的词
    摸进这儿   他奋力追赶自己的河底
                        成为它
    母亲飘散的白逆着美的方向
拓展噩耗   谁没目睹这首诗急急赶来
                粉碎
                辉煌如
                    我们的美学？

152

3. Poetic Inquiry – Another Embedded Voice

can't be real   is that beauty's fault?
                    imagine a shirt spread out on the riverbed
        steeping in the black of a Berlin night
                    imagine two eyes water-choked   mother choking on water
who says death isn't a drenched harmony?
    a little window on the riverbed lights up the show
    riverbed   a word that never stops leaping downwards
                            never stops finding leaked-out sobs
        leaves go down and wounds go up
            houses down   enjoyment of imminent snow goes up
tongue tip   is hooked ruin not enough by far?
                                imagine a self plunging down
            drowning in history's black water   plunging like a pebble
                there's no time other than a contraction of the lungs
                there's no grammar other than a shirt that strips life away
say   death's immeasurable side-on human shape
is filling up with sediment again still not enough?
                    in self-indulgent poetry there are only newly-arrived words
            touch in here   he does all he can to pursue his own river bed
                                        to become it
        mother's vaporizing white travels in the opposite direction to beauty
spreads the worst of news   no one saw this poem coming so quickly
                        shattering
                        dazzling as
                        our aesthetic?

四，超前研究

公元前二零零一年"九一一"那场雪
还没落下　　爬山虎凋成铁丝网
还圈住一九三三年大眼眶的眺望
石墙两侧的空都是余烬
天际撕开缺口　　每座塔灼伤着你塌两次
才听清一个东德士兵勒紧皮带的心
"No Tiananmen in my hand!"

　　一首诗的周年　　人群是铸铁的阴云

酝酿一个结晶的现实　　雪
隐身地下　　一串鲜嫩　　腐烂的念珠
数着你的手数玉辟邪体内一片白
我们的手　　伸出　　总离屠杀不远
　　又一个广场堆积肮脏萎缩的孩子
濡湿街角橡树　　小槐树　　橄榄树的根
和这里那里瞪着寒月的铜牌一起
和水做的柏林墙撬不开的铁门一起
一滴泪　　驱逐不认识的眼窝
　　一首诗着了火跃下　　却始终摔不进惊叫

　　　　　　　（波兹坦广场上
　　　　　年轻的夜色　　用化学味儿的精液
　　　　　　　喷绘一座城市　　覆盖一座城市
　　　　　　　　　　总是这座
　　　　　对称于脚下黑沙子吱嘎作响的公元前）

沿着刮不掉的舌苔走　　时间的固体
砸进你的固体　　沿着海平线
每秒钟缔造的字母　　被害的母亲令我们
重申被害　　沿着说了又说的凛冽
诗不得不在　　游乐场的笑声擦洗得晶亮
曼德尔施塔姆暴露着
　　　　　　每场雪都是初雪

154

4. Advanced Studies

2001 BC   September 11   that snow
still unfallen   ivy withered into barbed wire
still encircling a distant view of the great eye of 1933
space on either side of the stone walls filled with ruins
sky's edge tears a breach open   as each tower burns you collapse twice
then distinctly hear the heart of an East German soldier tightening his belt
'*No Tiananmen in my hand!*'

    a poem's anniversary   the throng is a dark cast-iron cloud

brewing a crystallised reality   snow
invisible underground   a string of fresh   rotten rosary beads
counting your hand-counted jades to ward off the white inside you
our hands   stretched out   never far from butchery
    another square heaped with dirty shrivelled children
soaks the street-corner oak   little locust tree   olive tree roots
with staring here and there at the bronze medal of the cold moon
with the iron gates a Berlin Wall made of water can't pry open
one teardrop   expels the unrecognizing eye socket
    a poem on fire jumps down   start to finish never plummets into screams

             (on Potsdamer Platz
       youthful dusk   with chemical-smelling liquids
           spray paints a city   covers a city
               always this one
     second person of the BC of black sand crunching underfoot)

walking along unscrapable tongue fur   the solids of time
smash into your solidity   along the skyline
letters created every second   murdered mothers make us
reiterate murder   stated and re-stated along bone-chilling cold
poetry can't but be there   playground laughter wiped sparkling clean
Mandelstam exposed
            each snow as the first snow

一首诗　　毁灭不尽地活着

一枚小小的六棱形不会过去　　它
舌尖挂着世界　　洒落的比世界更多
一扇小窗擎着我们相依走过的一侧
搂着决定不开枪像决定诗里一个词的东德士兵
涂抹进一首超前所有死亡的挽歌
公元前在诗句两头　　经霜　　红透　　掐紧
　　　　　　　　又一个吮含周年的星期天
一场银白的录制　　刺痛着无所不在
心　　抽搐一次已赢了历史

　　一首诗等到死者们逼真地回来

156

a poem   destroyed is indestructibly alive

a tiny hexagon can't go past   its
tongue snags on the world   its dribbling more than the world
a little window props one side of us up as we walk leaning together
choosing not to shoot as you pull the trigger like a DDR soldier picking a word
                                                            in a poem
scribbling into an elegy that transcends every death that has ever been
BC at both ends of a verse   suffering   utterly red   pinching
                        one more suck holds the Sunday anniversary
a silvery white recording   stings the all-pervading
heart   spasms once and has won history

    a poem waits until the dead come lifelike back

Notes on the poems

'Beds and Looms' – -*Chan* is a diminutive suffix used after a person's name or sometimes just the first-syllable of a person's name (or perhaps beloved pet animal's name) in order to show affection. -*Yan* is another diminutive suffix, used in Gunma dialect, to attach to a name, usually that of a man. The remainder of the poem contains a number of references to Japanese Buddhist culture. In Japan, Buddhist priests typically wear beautifully woven, ornately patterned robes requiring a high level of skill, and the town of Kiryū from which Arai comes, was known for producing them. The River of the Three Hells is the river separating the world of the living from the world of the dead in Buddhist mythology. The reference to Maria-Kannon comes from the premodern era, when Christianity was prohibited in Japan. During that time, a small minority of 'hidden Christians' clung to their beliefs and secretly used Buddhist images to practice their beliefs. For instance, they used the image of Kannon, the Buddhist goddess of mercy, as an image of the Christ's mother Mary. The words 'secret buddha' (*hibutsu*) are a euphemism for a woman's genitals. 'Form itself is emptiness, Emptiness itself is form' is a line from the Heart Sutra, one of the most commonly recited Buddhist texts.

'The Healds' – A heald frame is part of a weaving loom. The frame works to separate and lift some of the warp yarns above others, thus allowing the shuttle to pass through, holding the weft. Heald frames are rectangular and are supported by a set of thin wires called 'healds' or 'hettles'. Healds are attached to the frame vertically, and the threads move through their eyeholes while weaving. A 'magic lantern' (*gentō*) is something like an early slide projector, first developed in the seventeenth century, and directs light through small, rectangular slides onto a wall or screen. The word *kamaitachi* ('whirlwind') describes the cutting turbulent winds common in Japan's northern snow country. Traditional folk tales tell of weasel-like creatures that fly on whirlwinds slashing at human skin. In this poem, the focus is on the wind rather than this mythological creature. *Banzai* roughly translates as 'hurray' or 'long life', and when people say it, they often raise their arms over their heads. A warp beam is part of a loom. The ends of the warp threads are wound onto a warp beam roller at the back of the loom. A coiffeur (*kamiyui*) is someone who works as a hair dresser or barber, maintaining the complex hairdos women wore in traditional Japan.

'Come, Come, Fall Fast Asleep' – The title phrase 'come, come, fall fast asleep' (nen-nen korori yo) comes from a well-known Japanese lullaby. This poem was published in a major Japanese newspaper some months after the Fukushima meltdown when diagrams of the nuclear reactors were still appearing in the news on an almost daily basis.

'Ten Days of Blood' – Kim Koo was a Korean politician who fought for independence during the Japanese occupation. Yukdang was a Korean historian and leader of the independence movement during the Japanese occupation.

'Country Whore' – Kisaeng were entertainment artists who also often offered sexual services to the elite (*yangban*) for payment. Kisaeng were highly educated and well-read. They often held strong opinions about contemporary politics. Their clientele expected them to participate in intellectual debate. Although technically slaves who were often sold off by their families, they wrote poems, performed music, and enjoyed a greater degree of independence than most women in Korean society. With the increasing influence of Christianity and Western values in South Korea, the profession disappeared. However, prominent kisaeng throughout history are still revered for their beauty, independence, and acts of political rebellion. Their lives are often the subject of movies and tv shows. Yet, this has lead to the obfuscation of much of their memory. If not erased entirely from recorded history, their lives are often co-opted and white-washed into narratives of nationalism and patriarchy. Chokseoknu is a pavillion located inside Jinjuseong fortress and a gayakeum is a traditional string instrument.

'Dance: Swimming Naked with Li Bai' – Li Bai (701–762CE) doyen of Tang poets, was said to have drowned when he was drunk, reaching out from a small boat to grab the reflection of the moon on the water. Some say he died of consumption, or of drink, but no one knows. All we do know is that when he was granted a court appointment in 764, he was reported to have died more than a year before. Yang Lian's poem includes many allusions to Li Bai's poetry. An allusion to the famous lines of Tang dynasty poet Wang Han (fl. c.721CE), "Grape wine in a Nightgleam Cup / I want to drink, but the horseback lute is urging us on". The Nightgleam Cup was carved from jade from Gansu in the far northwest, which was said to glow in the dark. An allusion to the famous poem by Bai Juyi (772–846CE), 'The Ballad of Everlasting Sorrow', which describes the emperor's favourite concubine Yang Guifei performing a dance of this name. Li Bai was an intimate of the emperor, and is said to have drunk with him as Yang danced.

Advanced Study – The title derives from the title of the Berlin Wissenschaftskolleg (Institute for Advanced Study). 'mothers' hair that will never turn white again' is a quote from Paul Celan. The town of Ramallah is occupied by Israel. Palestinian writer Mourid Barghuti's famous line 'I saw Ramallah' describes the town and his own intense sense of exile. The poem references the long poem by Adonis entitled 'Concerto for 11th / September / 2001 B.C.'

Acknowledgements

We gratefully acknowledge permission to reprint copyright material in this book as follows:

Nouri Al-Jarrah
The translations are taken from *A Boat to Lesbos and other poems* (Banipal Books; 2018). The original poems were provided by the poet. Original poems © Nouri Al-Jarrah. Translations © Banipal Publishing.

Takako Arai
The translations are taken from *Factory Girls* (Action Books; 2019). The original poems were provided by the poet. Original poems © Takako Arai. Translation of 'When the Moon Rises' © Jeffrey Angles. Translation of 'Beds and Looms' © Jeffrey Angles. Translation of 'The Healds' © Carol Hayes and Rina Kikuchi. Translation of 'Shadows' © Jeffrey Angles. Translation of 'Come, Come, Fall Fast Asleep' © Jeffrey Angles.

Fawzi Karim
The translations are taken from *Incomprehensible Lesson* (Carcanet; 2019). The original poems were provided by the estate of the poet. Original poems © Fawzi Karim. Translations © Fawzi Karim and Anthony Howell.

Kim Yideum
The translations are taken from *Hysteria* (Action Books; 2019). The original poems were provided by Moonji Publishing Co. Original poems © Kim Yideum. Translations © Kim Yideum, Jake Levine, Soeun Seo and Hedgie Choi.

Judith Santopietro
The original poems and translations are taken from *Tiawanaku Poems from the Mother Coqa / Tiawanaku Poemas de la Madre Coqa* (Orca Libros; 2019). Original poems © Judith Santopietro. Translations © Ilana Luna.

Yang Lian
The translations are taken from *Anniversary Snow* (Shearsman Books; 2019). The original poems are provided by the poet. Original poems © Yang Lian. Translations © Brian Holton.

About the Poetry Translation Centre

Set up in 2004, the Poetry Translation Centre is the only UK organisation dedicated to translating, publishing and promoting contemporary poetry from Africa, Asia and Latin America. We introduce extraordinary poets from around the world to new audiences through books, online resources and bilingual events. We champion diversity and representation in the arts, and forge enduring relations with diaspora communities in the UK. We explore the craft of translation through our long-running programme of workshops which are open to all.

The Poetry Translation Centre is based in London and is an Arts Council National Portfolio organisation. To find out more about us, including how you can support our work, please visit: www.poetrytranslation.org.

About the Sarah Maguire Prize

The Sarah Maguire Prize for Poetry in Translation has been established in the memory of Sarah Maguire (1957-2017), the founder of the Poetry Translation Centre and champion of international poetry. The aim of the prize is to showcase the most exciting contemporary poetry from around the world, and to champion the art of poetry translation.

The prize will be awarded every two years for the best book of poetry from a living poet in English translation, published anywhere in the world. The winning poet and their translator(s) will divide a prize of £3,000. The 2020 inaugural edition of the prize was eligible to poets from Africa, Asia, the Middle East and Latin America, in forthcoming years the prize will be open to poets from anywhere beyond Europe.

Submissions to the 2022 edition of the prize will open in May 2021 and close in December 2021. Eligible entires must be published in 2020-2021 and submissions must be made by the publisher.

To find out more, please visit www.poetrytranslation.org/sarah-maguire-prize.